Varieties of
Southern
Evangelicalism

List of Contributors

J. WAYNE FLYNT is Chairman and Professor of History, Auburn University.

DAVID EDWIN HARRELL, JR. is Distinguished Professor of History, University of Arkansas.

SAMUEL S. HILL, JR. is Professor of Religion, University of Florida.

WILLIAM C. MARTIN is Professor of Sociology, Rice University.

MARTIN E. MARTY is The Fairfax M. Cone Distinguished Service Professor at the University of Chicago.

JOSEPH R. WASHINGTON, JR. is Professor of Religious Studies, University of Pennsylvania.

Varieties of
Southern
Evangelicalism

Edited by
David Edwin Harrell, Jr.

Foreword by
Martin E. Marty

Mercer University
Press
Macon, Ga. 31207

All books published by Mercer University Press are produced
on acid-free paper which exceeds the minimum standards set by the
National Historical Publications and Records Commission.

Library of Congress Cataloging in Publication Data
Main entry under title:
Varieties of southern evangelicalism.

"Essays . . . written by the participants in the Fourth Annual
Hugo Black Symposium held at the University of Alabama in Bir-
mingham in 1979"—Pref.
Includes bibliographical references and index.
1. Evangelicalism—Southern States: Congresses.   2. Southern
States—Religion—Congresses.
I. Harrell, David Edwin, Jr.   II. Hugo Black Symposium in Ameri-
can History (4th : 1979 : University of Alabama in Birmingham)
BR1643.U5V37   280'.4'0975   81-11312
ISBN 0-86554-015-2   AACR2

Contents

Preface

These essays were written by the participants in the Fourth Annual Hugo Black Symposium held at the University of Alabama in Birmingham in 1979. That conference was generously funded by the Alabama Committee for the National Endowment for the Humanities and the University of Alabama in Birmingham. All of the papers have been revised, and in one case the paper published here was delivered at an earlier conference on southern religion held at Auburn University. But in each case the author addresses the subject assigned to him for the Hugo Black Symposium.

We understood when we planned the symposium that we could not answer all questions about southern Evangelicals in one weekend, or in a short book of essays. The participants in the conference were requested to speak on the following specific questions: first, Martin Marty was asked to place southern Evangelicalism in a national context; second, we looked at the historical roots and general beliefs of three forms of southern Evangelicalism—the mainstream "southern church," sectarianism, and black religion. William C. Martin was asked to discuss the South's most famous religious son, Billy Graham. Finally, Samuel S. Hill, Jr., one of the most sensitive observers of southern religion, gave an overview of the varieties of modern southern Evangelicalism. This is clearly not all there is to be said about southern religion, but we hope the essays will give some new insight into the variety, regional uniqueness, and importance of southern evangelical religion.

The final editing of this manuscript was completed while the editor was a Fellow at the Institute for Ecumenical and Cultural Research in Collegeville, Minnesota—a beautiful and congenial haven. I am indebted to Virginia V. Hamilton, the architect of the Hugo Black Symposium and director of the first three conferences, who did much of the early work to secure funding for this symposium. I am particularly grateful to Dean George E. Passey of the University of Alabama in Birmingham, both for his initial financial support of the symposium and his continuing support in bringing this manuscript to its final form. Of course, the support of the Alabama Committee for the National Endowment for the Humanities was both generous and crucial. Mrs. Julia T. Sanders, an excellent student and friend, typed the manuscript in admirable haste. Portions of William C. Martin's essay appeared in *Texas Monthly* in March, 1978.

David Edwin Harrell, Jr.
Fayetteville, Arkansas

Foreword

The American Sunbelt has available a wide choice of pasts, so far as religion is concerned. Understanding most of them is urgent for anyone who wishes to deal with the American present. This book deals only with one complex out of that past, Southern Evangelicalism, but it appeared in the context of others.

The first of the religious pasts derives from the sixteenth century, when Spanish missionaries made their presence felt in Florida and today's Arizona, New Mexico, and Southern California. Their power was to wane in the course of time, but in the Southwest at least, natives and tourists find plenty of evidences of this Catholic presence. Those who thought that Hispanic America was something antique, nothing but a museum piece, were unprepared for the great *Völkerwanderung,* the migration of peoples which we are seeing in our own time. Today's Hispanic peoples may not feel themselves in direct continuity with the pioneers, but they come from the same religious background, share something of its ethos, and give new motives for studying that past.

A second available past was Establishment religion, which in the seventeenth century South meant Episcopalianism. Supported by law throughout the colonial era, this form of Christianity has also left its stamp on a part of the country, belongs to its antique shops, and rouses the curiosity of visitors to Virginia and the Carolinas. The Bruton Parish churches and their kind are among the prime monuments of the colonial past.

Episcopalianism was overwhelmed by revivalist churches after the Revolution, and today dominates nowhere in the South. It was disestablished at about the same time that it lost ground. But its churches are still prominent in many Southern cities. They offer alternatives to the more fervent Evangelicalisms described in this book. Most of all, they remind Americans of the ways in which, by law or custom, someone or other comes to dominate a region. In many a Southern city of today a fashionable Baptist church plays the role Episcopalianism once did. Establishment never quite dies.

Through those two centuries, the seventeenth and eighteenth, black religion in America got its start. Slave owners often grudgingly but later willingly began to share aspects of Christianity with their plantation hands, who later took their own nurture into their own agendas. Most of the blacks were members of churches that by genre belonged to the evangelical type. They borrowed freely from white churches and contributed more to the latter than these whites recognized. Today many of the great-great-grandchildren of those pioneers have moved to northern cities, but they dominate in much of the rural South. Many have begun to return with Sunbelt job markets to the prosperous cities. In any case, one would not pretend to understand the South or American religion without knowing the black churches. Their presence also forms a context for white Evangelicalisms of the sort described in this book.

A fourth available past to the South was the religion of the Enlightenment, which issued as much from Virginia as from anywhere. George Washington, Thomas Jefferson, James Madison, and their contemporaries ordinarily belonged to established Anglican churches and did their rounds of duty as vestrymen. Most of them, Jefferson sometimes excepted, spoke respectfully of Christianity, and believed in God. But this God took on the outlines of Deism's Supreme Being more than of Christianity's involved Father, and Jesus Christ was an exemplar of the divine more than a Savior. The Bible was a good book of conduct, but not of revelation. This form of religion is stamped into the legal tradition and many institutions of America, even though it was swamped and overwhelmed by the revivalists of the nineteenth century. It provided a foil for Evangelicals, who also profited from some of its contributions to religious freedom. It remains more than a monument from the past, and some of its arguments come back when Evangelicals argue for prayer in public schools. They derive the arguments for opposing "secular humanism" from founding fathers whose outlook today would be branded "secular humanism." That past is present.

This is not the place to exhaust the pasts: there are Mennonite and Lutheran pasts; there is a Jewish presence that dates far back to nineteenth century times. But these four samples show that Evangelicalism did not have the turf to itself; its triumph was not taken for granted. When the earliest Baptist and Methodist pioneers and circuit riders came to the scene where the other white establishments were already present, they were greeted about as warmly as a Unification Church or Hare Krishna recruiter would be on the premises of First Baptist Church in Dallas.

Yet they won their way, the hearts of the people, and the dominant position in southern religion. For the better part of a century and a half they tended to be looked down upon by the rest of the United States and Western European Christendom. They were written off as redneck by bluenose, as dirtpoor by landrich, as merely illiterate by Christians who were selectively illiterate (which means they could read but did not read religious texts), and/or as prejudiced by those who were prejudiced against them.

Today, for reasons that numbers of authors in the following pages describe, things have changed. Sunbelt prosperity has meant a new set of problems and possibilities for Evangelicalism. Its ethos attracts many who have been lured to the region. Meanwhile, the "country and westernization" of American culture has found its religious counterpart in the northward seepage of evangelical styles. Southerners, including the new Sunbelt arrivals, need to know the evangelical past to understand themselves and their neighbors. The rest of America, Canada, and Western Europe have to learn more in order to come to terms with their upstart neighbor in the American South. For if anywhere in the modern world religion and culture are bonded—whether on bleak dusty hilltops in remote reaches of Texas or in downtowns of the Dallases—it is in the Sunbelt. Reading books like this one may very well be an act that belongs in the survival strategy of informed people in many cultures. The new prosperous Evangelicalism did not just appear out of nowhere. It has roots that are tangled with many other subterranean forces. It has branches that entwine with non-religious branches under the Southern sky. I invite readers to pull up a rocker in the shade and begin a task of inquiry that will inspire more curiosities. This book is not an end, but a beginning.

Martin E. Marty

Introduction

David Edwin Harrell, Jr.

The twentieth century South has been a breeding ground of prophets. In the 1970s, Billy Graham, born in North Carolina, and Jimmy Carter of Plains, Georgia, were probably the two most widely-known evangelical Christians in the world. When President Carter was unseated in 1980 and returned home to reflect and work for God, one of the chief architects of his electoral defeat was evangelist Jerry Falwell of Lynchburg, Virginia, the founder of the Moral Majority movement and the nation's premiere spokesman for modern Fundamentalism. In addition to these most visible southern Evangelicals, the growth of American radio and television has given rise to a coterie of affluent evangelical celebrities with southern connections. In 1980 Oral Roberts was building a $120 million "City of Faith" in Tulsa, Oklahoma; James Bakker, host of a widely-viewed religious talk show, needed $100 million for his "Heritage Village" located not far from the birthplace of Graham; Pat Robertson, founder of the Christian Broadcasting Network of over 100 television stations, was headquartered in Virginia; television evangelist Kenneth Copeland had purchased 1,800 acres in Texas to build the "Revival Capital of the World" which would include a commercial-sized airport, a resort hotel, an amusement park, television and radio studios, and a retirement and "healing center;" and, in addition, there was pastor Rex Humbard of the Cathedral of Tomorrow in Akron, Ohio, who was reared in a family of itinerant Arkansas revivalists, and Jimmy Swaggart of Baton Rouge, Louisiana, and Kenneth Hagin of Tulsa, Oklahoma, and countless other independent salesmen of heart-felt religion and hope. Obviously, the recent resurgence of evangelical religion has been national and not southern—Graham has his headquarters in Minneapolis and such sounding names as Wheaton and Moody have no southern connotations. But the fact remains clear—evangelical Christianity feels particularly at home in the South. And southern boys have been the most successful prophets of the post-World War II period.

With the exception of the distinctive black religious experience in the South, there is little that is qualitatively unique about southern Evangelicalism. Southern evangelical churches and sects have parallels elsewhere in the country; southern religious thought is not marked by distinctive theological beliefs; southern religion addresses the same basic human problems as other religions.

But if the southern religious experience is not qualitatively distinct, it is quantitatively. Almost every student of the South has so asserted, often as a personal, subjective observation; recent surveys of public opinion lend objective support to this assumption. Southern Evangelicals have been more individualistic, less confident in social reform, more literal in their views of the Bible, more moved by personal religious experience; southern religion has been more given to sectarianism in the twentieth century—or so it is argued in this book. More obvious, the South has been the most solidly evangelical section of the country. Excluding the Mormon havens in Utah and Nevada, the most homogeneous religious states in the nation are in the South. The Bible Belt was a well entrenched stereotype by the early twentieth century, and it was one with clear substance to it.

Yet the story was never quite so simple. There are important differences among southern Evangelicals that defy generalization. Particularly important was the gulf between the open and friendly mainstream southern Evangelicalism and the more virulent types of southern sectarianism. The distance between Jerry Falwell and Billy Graham, or between snake handling Pentecostals and warmly saved Methodists was wide indeed, intellectually, culturally, and emotionally. Most Southerners were saved, and would readily tell you about it, but beyond that their testimonies varied widely in content and tone.

The molding of the soul of the South is a historical story. The section's unique regional history—its self-conscious encounter with slavery, and race relations, its defeat, its crushing poverty after the war, its bumpkin image—turned the South toward God. From this crucible of hardship and pain emerged the southern evangelical tradition. Progress finally came south after World War II, but it still has not displaced the entrenched southern confidence in prayer and preaching.

In the first article in this book Martin Marty reminds us that evangelical religion has been around for a good while and that, in spite of the predictions of its critics to the contrary, it is alive and thriving. In fact, says Professor Marty, Evangelicalism has been the characteristic way in which Protestants have related to the problems of modernity. The severity of these problems in the twentieth century explains the vitality of several forms of Evangelicalism in recent years.

Professor Marty's essay is full of insights. He explains some of the reasons why evangelical religion is particularly adapted to meet the needs of modern man in his "chopped up" environment, how it is the ultimate religion of "choice" and "intensity." Marty takes us through two stages of evangelical reactions to modernity. The evangelical revival during the first stage of modernity, stretching across nearly two centuries from Jonathan Edwards through the revivals of the nineteenth century, was more moderate than its twentieth-century successor, as the challenges of modernity were more moderate in those years. The evangelical momentum seemed to die in the twentieth century; in the South Bible-thumping Fundamentalism remained in the ascendancy but was regarded as anachronistic by most other Americans.

By the 1960s, Americans again felt pressed by a new modernity, a sense of dislocation more severe than before. Dissatisfied with the answers of liberal religion in the 1960s, most Americans looked to some form of traditional but evangelical religion. As Professor Marty says, old-time religion became avant-garde.

Perhaps this view can give us some insights into the prominence of the South in the modern evangelical revival. The South was a reservoir where the old-time message had remained intact amid the challenges of the twentieth century. Threatened by an intensified modernity in the postwar years, Americans looked for religious answers and Southerners had them. The South's role will remain large in the immediate American religious future, says Marty, "the real power and greater share in

American destiny will probably emerge from the course southern Evangelicals take."

The next three essays examine the historical roots of southern Evangelicals, and, in the process, speak of the diversity of the region's religion. Each of the essays, while grounded in conventional research, is written with an empathy based on familiarity. Each of the authors has heard the sermons and sung the hymns. Most Americans know the Elmer Gantry stereotype; most know the bizarre and outlandish extremes of southern religion; these essays tell something of its compelling heart. They look at what southern religion has done for southern people and at the simple but powerful message that Southerners taught their sons to teach the world.

Professor Wayne Flynt of Auburn University relates the story most familiar to Southerners. He writes about the "southern church," that common form of Evangelicalism shared by Southern Baptists, Methodists, and Presbyterians who compose 80 to 90 percent of southern church membership. The southern church was never monolithic, as Flynt shows, but it emphasized some common themes which have been influential in the formation of the southern mind and have been exportable in the post-World War II period.

Professor Flynt asks four questions about these mainstream southern Evangelicals: who are they, what do they believe, how did their religion speak to the needs of Southerners, and how did they use their religion to relate to society? The answers to those questions are not so simple as H. L. Mencken thought. For instance, argues Flynt, southern Evangelicals were deeply concerned about Christianizing the world around them, and that included cleansing society as well as saving individual souls.

My essay on the sectarian explosion in the South in the years after 1900 reveals another layer of southern Evangelicalism. In the twentieth century the mainstream evangelical churches of the South increasingly lost their most deprived members. For half a century the section became the nation's most prolific breeding ground for new sects: Pentecostals, Holiness, Church of Christ, and countless independent Baptists. The new sects seemed bizarre to most Americans, even to most southern Evangelicals, but they grew at an astonishing rate and, beneath their sometimes curious theologies, they reinforced the old values of southern Evangelicalism. The essay suggests some reasons why the sectarian revival erupted in the South around the turn of the century and examines the content of southern sectarian thought. Southern sects have been the most important single contributors to the vital resurgence of Fundamentalism in America and to the worldwide success of the charismatic movement.

Professor Joseph R. Washington, Jr. discusses "black folk religion" in an essay which shows both the kinship of black religion to the southern evangelical traditions and some distinctive differences. Washington acknowledges that there is much in the black experience that is shared by other humans, particularly, one might observe, by poor southern whites. And yet, the experience of American blacks, especially southern blacks, was different and so has black evangelical religion been different. With deep personal feeling Professor Washington sings the spirituals that sustained generations of blacks. And he finds in them not simple resignation and escapism but a fierce sense of black brotherhood and community. More than that, through all of the tragedy of the black experience, "joy and triumph" have remained the dominant theme of black religion. Whatever its shortcomings, writes Washington, black religion remains the best voice and the soul of the black community.

The next essay features the South's evangelical superstar, Billy Graham. Graham's roots are in the Southern Baptist tradition, and although international fame and glory have obscured his southernness, he is still looked on as a local boy who made good. William C. Martin's lively essay on Graham places the famous evangelist squarely in the middle of the American revivalistic tradition, the brightest star of the American system of voluntary religion. As Martin points out, Graham has gone nearly everywhere in the world and is far and away the most widely-known American religious figure. But Graham still likes to bring his crusades to such warm and God-fearing cities as Knoxville, Nashville, Jackson, Atlanta, and Shreveport. And if Billy Graham has grown since his early days in Bible schools, that also is a typical southern story.

Samuel S. Hill, Jr. concludes the book with a sweeping assessment of contemporary southern Evangelicals. Hill, a former minister and long-time sociological observer of southern religion, writes a personal, sensitive account of the variety within southern Evangelicalism. His story is, as he puts it, partly testimony, partly story telling, and partly preaching. The result is a probing of the "southern soul," or, as the reader will see, of the "southern souls." Hill lays bare the inner character of southern Evangelicals, the things they instinctively know about themselves and one another, and he tells personal stories that have almost universal meaning in the South. In all of this, and in his final plea, it is obvious whom Sam Hill likes and whom he dislikes, as it is obvious that his preferences do not reflect those of all Southerners, or all of the contributors to this volume.

Whatever one's likes or dislikes, here are some religious forms that are authentically southern Evangelical. They are rooted in southern experience, nurtured by southern customs, and have been exported in the post-World War II period with considerable success. It may be, as Sam Hill judges, that the forms of southern piety as they now exist have limited future use in the world, and even in the South. Or it may not be. It may be that the virulent, intense, individualistic forms of southern Evangelicalism will find new life because of the new challenges of modernity. Whatever the future, read on and you will learn something of who southern Evangelicals are, of how they came to be that, and why the world has taken a liking for their sons and made them prophets and presidents.

The Revival of Evangelicalism
and Southern Religion

Martin E. Marty

Ever since the 1730s, partisans of evangelical revivalism in American
Protestantism have spoken of its appearance in terms of surprise.
Jonathan Edwards set the pattern with his *A Faithful Narrative of the
Surprising Work of God etc.,* with its reports on awakenings in
Northampton and nearby towns in Massachusetts. In this pattern,
advocates insist that no social scientist may reduce the understanding of
their religious movement to the idea of "nothing but;" it is never to be
seen as "nothing but" a psychological eruption, a sociological freak, a
mere anthropological manifestation. "The beginning of the late work of
God in this place was so circumstanced that I could not but look upon it as
a remarkable testimony of God's approbation of the doctrine of
justification by faith alone," wrote Edwards in a preface to his published
series of sermons.[1]

From that "surprising" motif, moderns should draw two reminders.
First, the caution against reductionism is still in place. Attempts to

---

[1]See the facsimile of the original title page in C. C. Goen, ed., *The Great Awakening:
The Works of Jonathan Edwards*, vol. 4 (New Haven: Yale University Press, 1972), p.
128; the quotation from Edwards is on p. 19.

provide critical historical accountings of a movement need not exhaust all its meanings nor deprive it of rich spiritual and theological understandings. Second, the repeated presences of Evangelicalism based on revivals tend to take the form of surprising reappearances after times of decline and repeated prophecies of its permanent end. It surprises the skeptics and sometimes also its advocates by its durability.

To take but one example, William G. McLoughlin has both looked ahead to and back on the most recent previous period of high morale for Evangelicalism. The Brown University professor is by common if not universal consent among informed observers regarded as the best-equipped and most persistent chronicler of revivalism among those who write from an "outsider's" point of view in the American academy. In a position that he fashioned in the mid-sixties but did not publish until 1967, McLoughlin appraised the claim that Evangelicalism, growing out of revivals, might make up a new "third force" in Christendom alongside Catholicism and traditional Protestantism. He then dismissed this claim, choosing to see the religious resurgence of that period to be too pluralistic for such a picture. In any case, the new Evangelicalism was, he thought, too tied to the political right wing to survive its own new setback. "Probably the high-tide of this neo-evangelical 'third force' was the selection of Barry Goldwater as the Republican candidate for the Presidency in 1964." Everyone knew what happened to Goldwater and, hence, to his evangelical kissing kin. They had little future.[2]

Between 1967 and 1978, the various Evangelicalisms instead turned out to be the most aggressive and vital forces in American religion. Catholicism suffered after Vatican II and traditional or mainline Protestantism was dispirited and slipped statistically. But Evangelicalism, its hard-line counterpart in Fundamentalism, and its soft-line partner Pentecostalism knew prosperity. Yet McLoughlin in 1978 remained unconvinced that all of those made up a new "surprising work of God." A pluralistic revival of religion was indeed prospering, but it would not come to permanent focus in the evangelical sub-culture. Considerable ideology revealed itself in McLoughlin's view of the future: that in the 1990s it will be likely for a new consensus to emerge, one that will produce a fresh kind of political or civil religion and that will alter the

---

[2]William G. McLoughlin, "Is There a Third Force in Christendom?" *Daedalus* 96:1:61.

structure of American life insofar as that structure has been dependent upon Protestant evangelical awakenings. "Such a reorientation will most likely include a new sense of the mystical unity of all mankind and of the vital power of harmony between man and nature."

Over against a new kind of public pantheism McLoughlin posed the authoritarian and obscurantist fundamentalist leavings in the new Evangelicalism. "The current popularity of neo-Evangelicalism has led to the claim that 50 million born-again Christians are the avant-garde of the Fourth Great Awakening. This is hard to sustain." McLoughlin found evangelical Bible-centered faith to be attractive to millions of Americans, but Evangelicalism was too escapist, individualist, soul-centered, and unworldly to serve as the basis for a universal set of values for the culture.[3] He tended to reduce the surprising revival to the status of a social sub-culture, explicable in patent cultural terms.

Our task is not to play the game of what will win in the 1990s, nor are we called to put the new Evangelicalism in its place, as many secular historians do, or yield it the whole future, as do many of its advocates. We are to attempt to locate its place and power in ever-changing American society, especially in the context of the American South. Though I have an eye on the present and future, my accounting is historical and rests on this thesis: *Because Evangelicalism is the characteristic Protestant* (and, eventually and by indirection, Christian) *way of relating to modernity, it has recently experienced a revitalization concurrent with the development of a new stage of modernity.* This does not mean that Evangelicalism is epiphenomenal in relation to modernity, or that the modern condition predestines the outcome for passive religious adherents. Evangelicalism has been too inventive and assertive to make such an understanding look plausible. But there has been a symbiosis between unfolding modernity and developing Evangelicalism.

My one-sentence thesis demands and deserves unpacking, since inevitably one must employ terms in contexts that are not at first equally accessible to all. It includes at least four words that need some sort of definition.

By *evangelical*, I mean a Jesus-centered form of Protestantism that emerged during the last quarter millennium largely on Anglo-American

---

[3]William G. McLoughlin, *Revivals, Awakenings, and Reform* (Chicago: The University of Chicago Press, 1978), pp. 213-14.

soil. It is generated through the call for a turning from the old self and world, in a conversion through an intense experience of Jesus Christ by the power of the Holy Spirit. This conversion it reinforces with a fresh resort to biblical authority supported by high claims for the literal accuracy of the Bible. Evangelicalism then issues in a plea for ordered moral behavior and efforts to witness to and share the faith in the form of evangelism.

The reference to *Protestant* (and Christian) does not grant on any a priori basis to Evangelicalism its claim to be simply the whole of the faith once delivered to the saints. Even on a statistical basis, Evangelicalism is small compared to the Roman-Orthodox-Anglican-Lutheran complex. Temporarily, it made little if any mark in recognizable cultural and theological forms in most of the Christian centuries, when conversion was not so obvious a necessity for the survival of Christian community. Instead, historically it grew up on the soil of continental pietism and Moravianism and then emerged in Puritan, Methodist, and specialized "evangelical" and primitive movements in Anglo-America and, henceforth, "in all the world." When referring to its indirect role in larger Christianity, I imply the fact that Roman Catholicism in a voluntary society both instinctively and by borrowing adopted much of the evangelical style and some of its content. This derivative evangelical Catholicism was apparent in nineteenth century Catholic revivalism, whose story is only now being told,[4] and in twentieth century Catholic Pentecostalism.[5]

Third, *revitalization* refers to a construct that, with McLoughlin, I borrow from anthropologist Anthony F. C. Wallace, and carry over from "primitive" society into complex ones like our own. Revitalizations grow out of widespread understandings of individual stress, periods of cultural distortion when the old ways no longer work, followed by nativist or traditionalist movements within the culture to restore its beliefs, values, and behavior patterns. Then comes the development of new world views or "mazeways" by which individuals and finally the culture find their way toward new syntheses. More than McLoughlin, however, I see innovative

---

[4]Jay P. Dolan, *Catholic Revivalism: The American Experience, 1830-1900* (Notre Dame: The University of Notre Dame Press, 1978).

[5]The literature on this subject is enormous; for a sample, see Joseph H. Fichter, *The Catholic Cult of the Paraclete* (New York: Sheed and Ward, 1975).

power in appeals to traditional forms. Reworked, they can revitalize a culture and need not lead to cultural Byzantinism or ossification. Because McLoughlin looks for revitalization of the *whole* culture on an almost unitary model, he has to see Evangelicalism as but part of one wave, a passing stage toward a larger and more creative whole. Because I see modern societies like America more as a cluster of sub-cultures in search of but not necessarily finding a post-pluralist integrative culture, awakenings in sub-cultures—some of them perhaps forty or fifty million citizens strong—are more impressive to me. I do share with McLoughlin more sense of the limits of evangelical scope than do triumphalists in the evangelical movements.[6]

The reference, fourth, to new stages of *modernity* is to post-World War II America with its culture dominated increasingly by electronic communication, rapid transportation, mobile and kinetic styles of living, affluence, and a sense of entitlement in large publics. All of these factors place new demands on traditional religion, which has shown marvelous abilities to adapt. Sometimes the adaptation is evolutionary, in continuity with the content of old symbols; at times it is revolutionary, wrenching as it does utterly new meanings from old symbols. To take but one illustration: when Evangelicalism was the voice of dissent or of the disaffected, its call to conversion in Christ meant a call to turn one's back on the world. In the recent surge, prosperous Evangelicalism still uses the language of a call to turn one's back on the world. But it now serves as a means of providing ritual process for applicants to the approved world, in a day when the President of the United States, business leaders, celebrities, athletes and beauty queens, and civic figures attribute their worldly success to the fruits of conversion.[7] The symbols "world" and "convert" remain constant but their content has been drastically changed by an improvising set of leaders and respondents.

Now, it may seem quirkish to see Evangelicalism, "the old-time religion," as the most adaptive and inventive new ("Modern") faith, but maybe we should not be so surprised at this. Through the years of the first evangelical stirrings, its parties received names like New Light, New Side, and New Schools, even if at times the opponents of these parties—

---

[6]McLoughlin, *Revivals*, pp. 9-17.

[7]For documentation of several sorts of "worldliness," see Richard Quebedeaux, *The Worldly Evangelicals* (New York: Harper and Row, 1978).

one thinks of proto-unitarians like Charles Chauncy and Jonathan Mayhew in Massachusetts—were enlightened rationalists of a sort, "moderns" in the eyes of intellectual historians. Here it is important to make a distinction on one hand between the modern*ism* of the Chauncys and their nineteenth century counterparts who received the name The Modernists, and, on the other, these evangelical exemplifiers of modern*ity*. Modernism was at heart a movement that called for open adaptation to the new worlds of science, nature, and reason; it called for a synthesis of Christ and culture even to the point that Christianity lost its own initiatives. If modernity is different than modernism, what is it?

Modernity exemplifies at least three characteristics in this context. First, in colloquial sounding language, it refers to the *"chopping up"* of life, and of the functions and understandings of religion in life. Historians are wary of deterministic sociological schemes of religious evolution, so we shall use them with care. Yet it is fair to picture "pre-modern" existence as characterized by more nearly wholistic approaches to life. Lines between sacred and profane developed, but there was evidently less confidence that the profane or secular had true independent or autonomous standing beyond the realm of the unseen spirits who dominated all of life. Rather than trace the whole development of modernity, let me quote a pithy condensation by John Murray Cuddihy. Modernity means differentiation ("chopping up"):

> differentiation of home from job; the differentiation of political economy (Marx) into politics and economy; differentiation of the culture system from the personality and social systems; differentiation of economy from society (Weber and Parsons and Smelser); differentiation of fact from value, of theory from praxis; differentiation of art from belief.
>
> Differentiation is the cutting edge of the modernization process, sundering cruelly what tradition had joined. It separates church from state (the Catholic trauma); it produces the 'separated' or liberal state, a limited state that knows its 'place,' differentiated from society. Differentiation slices through ancient primordial ties and identities, leaving crisis and 'wholeness-hunger' in its wake.[8]

---

[8]John Murray Cuddihy, *The Ordeal of Civility: Freud, Marx, Levi-Strauss, and the Jewish Struggle with Modernity* (New York: Basic, 1974), pp. 9-10.

Evangelicalism ministers to the hunger for wholeness, but is itself based on the differentiation model. It relishes separation of church and state, in the main has argued that religion should not meddle in politics and should abandon the social sphere, and has concentrated on the private dimensions of life in a voluntaryistic church mold.

Not that evangelicalist triumphalism has no desires to smuggle Catholic understandings in the back door behind its "separationist" facade. Thus some Baptists who argue for the separation of church and state might be the strongest advocates for prayer in the public school, as if a universal base for prayer could be found in society. They know that with "majority rule" in evangelical communities the faith of the civic institution would be Evangelicalism. But this reveals a cultural inconsistency born of nostalgia for the pre-Evangelicalism world or for the cultures of evangelical dominance. Who does not like to have power and monopoly? In practice, Evangelicalism was born at the moment when the understanding that religion passed through the genes or came with the territory—the old model of Christendom—was disintegrating. With genius it chose to specialize by differentiating portions of life. Evangelicalism concentrated in private vices and virtues, saving souls even at the expense of care for the whole life of humans, seeing the ecclesiastical sphere as one of special concentration on private, leisured, familial, and personal life no matter what happened to political, social, or cultural meanings.

Alongside this sense of "chopped-upness," modernity produced and Evangelicalism creatively exploited and exploits voluntaryism or *choice*. David Apter, who sees the roots of modernity especially in economic choice has spelled this out:

> The dynamic aspect of modernization . . . can be expressed in the general proposition that modernization is a process of increasing complexity in human affairs within which the polity must act. . . . Personal meaning and social meaning; the rhythm and pace of social activity; the roles of the misfit and the innovator; the hierarchy of power and prestige; concern with interpersonal associations, political ideology, religion—each of these implies a different pattern of desire, motive, and choice. . . . Modernization as the process leading to the state of modernity, begins when man tries to solve the allocation problem. . . . Self-conscious concern with choice has led to an

attitude of experiment and invention that has changed man's entire outlook. . . . Hence, in these times, more than ever before, it is not only interesting but also important to recognize this characteristic of modernity: Choice.[9]

The Evangelicals of 1734 and, say, 1968 alike discerned this feature of modernity while established religion in the earlier period and adapted religion in the later one did not. The National Council of Churches through its social engagements in recent decades has acted as if it is an established church, entrenched and inescapable as a moral voice in the society. Evangelicalism took pains to recruit people, to ask them to make a choice, and even to find "the church of their choice," which became a locale for a new kind of power, albeit a specialized form.

From the First Great Awakening to recent Evangelicalism the impulse to choose has been strong. Billy Graham most successfully calls for decisions for Christ by voluntary agents and characteristically calls his magazine *Decision*. Christendom (and Judaism) did not call for "decision;" religion was passed through the genes, through the loins of godly parents.[10] It did "come with the territory." Theologians, of course, may discern behind the language of grace in evangelical Protestantism some of the old Pelagian nuances of merit and achievement. One thinks of the "I Found It!" bumper stickers as the direct opposite of Protestant evangelical understandings of divine initiative. But the initiated knew how to translate this symbol of successful choice and integrate it into their grace system.

In this view, it was not mere coincidence that Evangelicals came along at the beginning of the modern period of economics. Adam Smith was also an eighteenth century person. There were good reasons for it to emerge during the rise of the voluntary political system of which anti-evangelical Thomas Jefferson was an agent, or of the early industrial capitalist period where the choices Apter describes became urgent. Alfred North Whitehead was correct when he saw Evangelicals as people of genius when they made direct intuitive appeals to the hearts of new

---

[9]David Apter, *The Politics of Modernization* (Chicago: The University of Chicago Press, 1965), pp. 3, 5, 6, 10.

[10]See Edmund Morgan, *The Puritan Family: Religion and Domestic Relations in Seventeenth-Century New England* (New York: Harper and Row, 1966), p. 182; the phrase is Increase Mather's, from a sermon of 1678.

industrial classes in England and frontier people in America.[11] The Evangelicals are the pioneer religious moderns, with their pietist *ecclesiola in ecclesia*—the chosen little church inside the given great big surrounding one—as a model. They still remain in the avant-garde in the electronic age as they adopt the most rigorous secular advertising and entertainment styles for the gathering of television clienteles, the final development of "chosen" religion.

The third feature of modernity in religion is *intensity.* Moderns who are to be attracted at all want their religion to be "hot." If it is to be portable and personal, it cannot trade on footnotes in libraries or rely on scholarly elites. It must be accessible and instantly open to experience and interpretation by common people in the industrial city, on the frontier, or in the suburb. While liberal religion has lived off the capital earlier generations invested in the realm of experience, Evangelicalism insists that the immediate experience of the prophets and saints and mystics can come to the object of revivals. Thus was born what Perry Miller calls "the rhetoric of sensation."[12] calculated to give the "hot" experience. Then followed the contrived "means" of the era of Charles Grandison Finney.

As with experience, so with authority: for chopped up and chosen religious life there must be intense or "hot" understandings, usually in the form of an infallible and unambiguous Bible. Here appear no nuances of ecclesiastical hierarchy, no subtleties of scholarship, but, far more than in the original Reformation, there are insistences that a clear and unerring God must speak clearly, unerringly, and without contradiction or ambiguity in the code book of his revelation, the Bible. With this hot understanding came other assets necessary for moderns: the ability to maintain boundaries, something which cannot easily be done on the basis of ambiguous or controverted understandings of scripture. All must be deposited, secure, closed in, yet accessible to ordered and repentant minds. In modern crisis, this set of understandings originally prospers at the expense of more reserved and restrained ones, and thus in times of identity diffusion such as recent decades have produced, Evangelicalism saw new openings.

Modernization in these terms is not a simple, one-way process without counteractions or trends. Cuddihy can speak of

---

[11]Alfred North Whitehead, *Adventures of Ideas* (New York: Mentor, 1955), pp. 30ff.

[12]Perry Miller, *Errand into the Wilderness* (Cambridge, Massachusetts: The Belknap Press of Harvard University Press, 1956), pp. 167ff.

"demodernization" or "dedifferentiation" through ideology and force, as in the case of Marx and Mao. They ministered to "wholeness-hunger" by developing an encompassing outlook that overcame the chopping up of the realms of life and minimized if they did not remove all choice.[13] Similarly, there can be episodes in history in which spiritual forces give special attention to new problems and opportunities posed by developing modernity. It is possible to speak of the older Evangelicalism developing against the background of "Modernity 'A'" and after a pause, the new one emerging in the midst of "Modernity 'B'."

Modernity "A" was the period of the industrial, capitalist, and democratic revolutions of the eighteenth century. John Wesley, George Whitefield, and Jonathan Edwards's and their aftermath, of course, were not pondering religious solutions to the problem of alienation in the era of factories. Edward's Northampton was a quiet little town and Whitefield had successes on the back roads. But their style, in most cases itinerant, and the claim by Wesley that "the world is my parish," were posed over against the older notion that "my parish is the world," as it was in territorial Christendom. Evangelicals thus revealed their ability to minister to new spiritual needs. Where there was not itineracy and where the parish remained "the world," it was necessary to intensify the experience of Jesus Christ so that people knew conversion while staying in their immediate context.

Yet the first response was moderated by several factors. "Chopping up" of life was not fully developed at once because of the relative homogeneity of the population in Protestant, and especially white Protestant, America of British provenance. Southern white civilization remained especially homogeneous through the nineteenth century. The element of "choice" was not so drastic in a day when relatively similar evangelical forces competed for a common market; they crowded the center theologically. When an Evangelical Alliance was formed, continentals and Britishers were attracted to it, but not a few visitors observed that Americans did not take to the Alliance because they did not need one. They were already allied, were strangely similar across church lines. And the matter of "hot" or intense experience, while it stirred great controversy, still drew less notice than it would in an era which prophets had denominated secular or cool about religious stirrings.

---

[13]Cuddihy, *Ordeal of Civility*, p. 10.

The First and Second Great Awakenings and even the 1857-58 lay revivals in American cities were part of this moderated modernity. Strains, however, came during the century after the lay revival. Between it and 1908, when the Federal Council of Churches was formed, American Protestantism developed a two-party system on matters social, with the more conservative Evangelicals tending to deal more with the private dimensions of faith. They had "chopped up" life and were so settled in this new pattern that they made the more liberal factions look like innovators for simply trying to regress to wholistic medieval models. Meanwhile, the challenges by biological evolution and higher criticism to the Protestant theological synthesis, accompanied by the rise of an adaptive Modernist party, led a large element of Evangelicalism to turn to hard-line resistance in the movement called Fundamentalism, which crested and was apparently defeated around 1925. After that date the more intransigent versions of Evangelicalism were supposed to have retreated in disgrace, to become fossilized or at least to remain on cultural bypaths. Instead some of the children of Fundamentalism regrouped, learned some new civility, and came to fresh understandings of the modern assaults and opportunities. And the old strain of Evangelicals who had never even been in the frontline fight against Modernism and who therefore could keep a more open and flexible style, began to reemerge in the 1940s as organized "neo-Evangelical" parties. The 1950s saw Billy Graham relate to a new stage of modernity, and soon ethical leaders and intellectuals emerged to give new definition.

During the interlude between 1925 and the mid-fifties, a number of threats posed themselves to Evangelicalism. Some thought it might wane and virtually disappear. Thus British Evangelicals of the Clapham Sect sort had been followed by generations of ever-declining church involvement and the rejection by their own young. Individuals could also commute between value systems. They might retain their minute membership in Evangelicalism but "pass" in the larger culture. Third, they might institutionalize themselves in new denominations, Bible schools, publishing and broadcasting enterprises, and the like. Or, fourth, they might sustain themselves and wait for revitalization in congregations and in the mainline denominational underground. All four of these happened between 1925 and, say, 1952.

Evangelicalism in many minds came to be lumped with Fundamentalism, and was mentally located in the Bible Belt of the South. In what others saw as cultural backwaters it prospered, but few thought it could erupt from there until Billy Graham and his kind brought new respectability. In short, Evangelicalism endured. Then, just before its most ambitious flowering, it encountered cultural shock of many sorts in the 1960s. Activists stole the media limelight. An era of the prophets of a new secularity emerged; heirs of the late Dietrich Bonhoeffer or Teilhard de Chardin, they pictured the demise of the symbol systems that Evangelicals cherished, rich as these were in miracle and metaphysics, mysticism and meditation. "God is dead" did not promise much for the evangelical cause!

Far-seeing thinkers then made desperate attempts to "demodernize." Thus Sidney E. Mead and Robert Bellah led the ranks of those who looked for wholistic civil or republican faiths which might help people transcend the "chopped up" life of the denominations.[14] Interfaith, ecumenical, and semi-secular thinkers, by celebrating this civil sphere or the religions of world integration, set out to minimize choice, albeit without necessarily trying to impose coercion in their utopias. And intensity seemed out of fashion as Harvey Cox asked for a moratorium on God-talk, in the spirit of Bonhoeffer who had called for diffidence in speaking about religious experience.[15] Clearly the emergence of such a "non-religious" religion bode ill for Evangelicalism, but it also did not satisfy the religious needs and interests of people as they faced "Modernity 'B'."

Modernity "B" posed new needs. First among these was for personal identity in a time of diffusion, of confusion over social location, of bewilderment over the questions, "Who am I?" and "To whom do I belong?"[16] Evangelicalism, by forming a new community and using its code-words about conversion and biblical authority, helped provide boundaries for the psyche.

Second, the new modernity called for fresh interpretations of the world of Americans whose system—witness Vietnam and Watergate—seemed no longer to be full of promise. Millennial language now reappeared, and believers looked for the promise of personal rewards in a

---

[14]See the essays by Bellah, Mead, and others in Russell E. Richey and Donald G. Jones, *American Civil Religion* (New York: Harper and Row, 1974).

[15]Cuddihy discusses Bonhoeffer on this theme, *Ordeal of Civility*, pp. 235, 237-38.

[16]For a psychological accounting, see Robert Jay Lifton, *Boundaries: Psychological Man in Revolution* (New York: Macmillan, 1967).

society they could not change on any large scale. Over against the impersonal administrative styles of management in state and commerce and church, there rose a generation of people who enjoyed immediate experiences. Some of them chose mind-expanding drugs or fashionable therapies; many "turned East." But the largest wave of experiencers were in traditional forms of Judaism, Catholicism, and most of all in Protestant Evangelicalism.

What issued from the encounter with Modernity "B" is what I would call an "ultramodern" adaptation, in which Evangelicals are again the avant-garde, the "old-time religion" being the most modern and new of all. Thomas Luckmann's *The Invisible Religion*[17] has described the structure of this period. Religion now became a matter of final "chopping up" into utter differentiation and a world in which mediating structures play little part. There came to be as many religions as there were people. The electronic church ministers to this situation, since it generates no tangible congregation, only clienteles of people who converge on a set of signals.

Ultramodernity further enhances choice, for the clienteles are not content with even the maze of denominational inheritances. Each denomination is chopped in two and one must choose this party or that. That division is only the beginning. Each must also choose a caucus, a cause, a movement, a celebrity, until these all come to compete with the congregations and denominations. The ultramodern solution certainly generates intensity, "hot" experiences. One is "into" Pentecostalism or the Jesus movement, an evangelical commune or a charismatic healing group, each of which has its passwords and argot, its rules of behavior and sectarian sets of meanings. Mainline Christianity has been puzzled by the new demands made on faith in the ultramodern world, but Fundamentalists, Pentecostals, and Evangelicals thrive on them and in their midst.

The question of *communitas*, profound community and social control, is left over in the newest adaptation. What is ahead? Once again, there may be large-scale dropouts and wanings, as there were after British Evangelicalism's prime in Modernity "A". There may be more commutation than before between worlds, as some mainliners acquire

---

[17]Thomas Luckman, *The Invisible Religion: The Problem of Religion in Modern Society* (New York: Macmillan, 1967).

evangelical traits and various evangelical groups go looking for "catholic roots." In the circulation of elites, many Evangelicals may become so adapted as to turn mainline; it is hard to be marginal when one of your own is president of the United States and all the worldly celebrities are in your camp. Or the movement may represent a longer-scale revitalization if it is well anchored in the congregations.

What does all this have to do with the southern religious theme which occupies the other writers in this collection?

Historically, southern Evangelicalism matches this two-stage or two-episode approach. It was shaped during Modernity "A," a period which saw the established Episcopal Church lose ground. Blacks and whites together in the Second Great Awakening found Evangelicalism most to their liking. During the interlude period, southern Evangelicals were not asleep. They had succeeded in stamping southern faith with the outlooks and behavior patterns of the older Evangelicalism and took as their foil not only European radical Christian thought but even the more moderate novelties of northern American "brain-working" families and scholars.

But "Modernity 'B' " has seen sudden new prosperity for the evangelical cause. The South is the new center of mobility and affluence, of electronic and technological hunger and capability in the aerospace age. Demographic trends favor southern Evangelicalism over all comers and the face of new comers. At this time of drastic social change, the people of transition did what pioneers have often done: they looked backward, taking symbols from the past to legitimate and inform the cultural moves they make. They are vulnerable to the charge that they are turning success-minded and worldly.

Those of us who share many of the assumptions of the evangelical world but are listed as being on its margins, and those of us who by accident of birth and vocation do not live in the South, are watching southern Evangelicalism in the face of "Modernity 'B' " with special interest. Let the media deal with the more exotic and esoteric Eastern-based occult and cultic movements; the real power and the greater share in American destiny will probably emerge from the course southern Evangelicals take. If they should regress, as it were, to intransigent forms during the *Battle for the Bible*, they are likely to become very strong in a defined sub-culture. If they should consolidate some of their gains made along the lines of ultramodern appeals, by converting them to stronger communal and congregational life—as they do in many locales—it is likely that the sub-culture will be less well defined but more potent. It may well be that Evangelicals could then burst the bounds of the sub-culture and be taken more seriously in the larger culture. This is not to say that Evangelicals should seek the potential of such impact or the implied favor that comes with it. It is possible, however, that if they do not turn merely worldly and success-minded, if they are ready to forego the impulse to gain the whole world at the expense of losing their collective soul, they might indeed turn out to be seeking the kingdom. And all kinds of things can be added as surprising benefits along the way.

One in the Spirit, Many in the Flesh: Southern Evangelicals

Wayne Flynt

Recovering American religious history is imperative if we are to understand the way in which Americans thought about human nature and destiny. Church historian Samuel S. Hill, Jr., focusing specifically on the South, has maintained that the solidarity of religion is as important as politics and race to southern distinctiveness. No other region has been so uniformly evangelical Protestant. In the 1960s membership in Baptist and Methodist churches constituted nearly 80 percent of the total church affiliation in six southern states. Adding Presbyterians and Disciples of Christ, the total in Alabama for the four evangelical churches was 90.9 percent of the total, 88.3 in Arkansas, 93 in Georgia, 93.9 in Mississippi, 87.5 in Tennessee.

Obviously, any serious attempt to understand the southern mind must begin by grappling with the region's Evangelicals, and this task is not easy. One observer of the southern church in the 1920s wrote with more perplexity than insight: "Religion in the South is infinitely puzzling. It is a paradox, dead and yet alive, unprogressive and narrow but a powerful force."

This paper asks four questions: (1) Who are southern Evangelicals? (2) What do they believe? (3) What function did religion serve for them?

(4) What was their approach to culture? Like most academicians, I have more answers than questions, so I limit this discussion to white Evangelicals who have organizational roots in the Protestant Reformation, namely Baptist, Methodists, and Presbyterians.

Who Are Southern Evangelicals?

Defining mainstream southern Evangelicals is not as easy as it first appears. In the late eighteenth century they were mainly economically insecure frontier folk with a strong bias against the aristocracy. The Anglican church with its commitment to the upper class sought to perpetuate a hierarchial social system. Powerless common people came to despise the established church and condemned the sins they associated with the social class it represented: horse racing, gambling, slavery. Southern folk religion became a volatile, defiant movement of alienated lower middle class and lower class whites. Nor was the animosity one-sided. Upper class communicants in the Episcopal church had no use for the theology or character of Evangelicals. One aristocratic Virginian described Baptists in unflattering terms: "Some of them were hair-lipped, others were blear eyed, or humpbacked, or bow-legged, or club-footed; hardly any of them looked like other people."[1]

Of course, not every frontiersman was religious. In 1800 only one in fifteen Americans was a church member, and religious literacy, especially on the southern frontier, was astonishingly low. A piece of religious folklore described a preacher's witness to a woman in a remote backwoods cabin. Asked if she had any religious convictions, she replied: "Naw, not my ole man, neither. He was tried for hog stealing once, but he warn't convicted."

No wonder the Evangelicals attacked the frontier with such fierce determination. Circuit riders and missionaries led revivals which saved the souls and changed the lives of tens of thousands. By 1850 an estimated one in seven Americans belonged to a church, twice the percentage of fifty years earlier.

But the intervening years had also changed southern Evangelicals. No longer were they primarily powerless, defiant, lower class folk. Many of them had become small planters or prosperous yeoman farmers. Although a disproportionate share of wealth and political power still

---

[1]Walter B. Posey, *The Baptist Church in the Lower Mississippi Valley, 1776-1845* (Lexington: University of Kentucky Press, 1957), p. 2.

resided in the hands of Episcopalians, the Evangelicals shared enough to become conservative defenders of much that they had criticized earlier, including slavery. By the 1830s, few southern Evangelicals raised their voice in protest against the "peculiar institution," and by 1844-45 they had repudiated the increasingly anti-slavery stance of their northern brethren and established their own ecclesiastical organizations.

More subtle changes occurred during the same years. Bonds of professionalism grew among ministers. More of them attended college and afterwards established academies to train their children and those of their parishioners. Denominational colleges mushroomed and ecclesiastical bureaucracies developed to manage tract societies, home and foreign mission agencies, denominational newspapers and the other trappings of organized religious life.

Not all Evangelicals made the transition into affluence. The result was internal class divisions which matched the earlier cleavage between Episcopalians and Evangelicals. These differences resulted in the birth of the Disciples of Christ and the Cumberland Presbyterian church, and animosity between missionary, anti-missionary, and Landmark Baptists. Although these controversies had theological dimensions, class elements were more significant. In most cases the dissenters were poor and mountain whites, those closer to the frontier experience who resented the increasing religious sophistication of their wealthier and more politically powerful lowland brothers. The Calvinistic antimission Baptists objected to all human means of conversion, believing that the sinner's fate was in the hands of God alone. They rejected revivals, missionary and tract societies, and church discipline in matters of drinking and personal vices. They especially resented educated missionaries who came to the mountains and moralized about how quaint and backward the Primitive Baptists were. By 1844 there were some 900 antimission preachers, 1,622 churches, and 68,000 members. For the next fifteen years a battle raged within southern folk religion, especially in the Piedmont and Mountain counties, which left permanent marks on the folk religion of the South.[2]

---

[2]Bertram Wyatt-Brown, "The Antimission Movement in the Jacksonian South: A Study in Regional Folk Culture," *The Journal of Southern History* 36 (November 1970): 501-29; and Wyatt-Brown, "Religion and the Formation of Folk Culture: Poor Whites of the Old South," in *The Americanization of the Gulf Coast, 1803-1850,* Lucius F. Ellsworth, ed. (Pensacola: Historic Pensacola Preservation Board, 1972), pp. 20-33.

The years from the Civil War to the Second World War were difficult ones for most Evangelicals in the South. Many rural churches combined middle class and poor in a fellowship of mutual acceptance. Congressman Brooks Hays, a former president of the Southern Baptist Convention who lost his seat in the House of Representatives because of his courageous stand for racial moderation during the Little Rock desegregation crisis, described the democratic congregation of his boyhood in Russellville, Arkansas:

> In Western Arkansas at the turn of the century, the typical congregation covered the whole spectrum of community life. There was an admirable reflection of it in the emphasis upon equality. My first Sunday School teacher was a blacksmith. Later I was instructed by a coal miner, whose gnarled hands symbolized for me the hardships of the period's life. There sat on the same pew with my parents the woman who did my mother's washing. "Miss Helen," mother called her. Her vote in church conference had the same weight as my mother's and father's, and her presence on that third pew with them remains for me an authentic symbol of Baptist democracy.[3]

In larger towns, however, internal class divisions became pronounced. "Up town" churches catered to middle class merchants and professionals and maintained little contact with their co-religionists in mill town. Most industrial workers—miners, textile mill workers—if religious at all, were Methodists or Baptists. But then, so were their bosses. After 1900 urban churches developed greater interest in labor problems, but neglected the plight of churches in the rural areas.

Since World War II, southern Evangelicals generally have enjoyed unprecedented prosperity, and most have moved into the middle class. Their support of the economic and social status quo is well known. Brooks Hays noted that his childhood Baptist church in Russellville, Arkansas, had moved to a more prominent corner and served a more prosperous constituency. A newer Baptist church, following less formal ways, now serves the town's poorer folk. Yet, the diversity that developed in the nineteenth century remains, primarily in the rural-urban dichotomy that is so basic to understanding modern American culture.

---

[3]Brooks Hays, "Reflections on the Role of Baptists in Politics and the Future of America," *Baptist History and Heritage* 11 (July 1976): 170.

More than any denominations, southern Methodists and Baptists remained powerful among poor whites in the rural South. Of the 35,000 Southern Baptist churches in 1977, 14,000 were rural and 4,000 more were in villages of less than 500 people. Many of the churches were small; 69.4 percent of all Southern Baptist churches enrolled less than 300 members in 1977.[4]

Obviously, southern Evangelicals changed and diversified between 1800 and 1977. The perceptions of reality, class interests, and the proper function of religion differed greatly between Evangelicals who were scratching out a subsistence life in the remote mountains of Appalachia and their brothers-in-Christ who taught at the University of North Carolina or owned banks in Birmingham. The differences still exist even after the homogenizing effect of post-1945 affluence.

What Do Evangelicals Believe?

What do southern Evangelicals believe? They constitute a "southern church" with a common ideology forged in the early years of the nineteenth century. Until 1800 theology in the South was as varied as in other American regions; but in the next three decades southern Evangelicals developed remarkably similar patterns of thought, different in some ways from their European theological roots.

The initial element in this process was the second Great Awakening, which gained fame on the Kentucky frontier at Cane Ridge and spread rapidly. Sectarian differences were temporarily put aside for oneness of the spirit.

Despite the emotional extremes and social eccentricities of the revivals, (more souls were made than saved was the common charge), they produced a remarkably enduring set of characteristics. Rather than viewing the camp meetings as essentially a social event with a thin religious veneer, one should view them as the anvil upon which plain folk religion was forged. The common people who preached and exhorted without benefit of much education made folk religion democratic. The camp meeting songs, which were both rousing and easily sung, contained a coherent system of religious symbols important to frontier people. Appeal was to the heart more than to the head, and conversion was the dominant religious experience. The quest for personal holiness which followed conversion took an individualistic course; reform was inward

---

[4]*The Quarterly Review* 38 (July-August-September 1978): 10-11.

and aimed at the individual, not outward and aimed at society. Theology was heavily laced with Calvinistic notions of the sinfulness of man and the need for repentance. Services were less liturgical, reliance on Biblical authority more complete, the importance of good, popular preaching greater than was true among other American Protestants.[5] These elements became the essence of southern folk religion.

Some of these elements are so important as to demand elaboration. Democracy was both the chief strength and weakness of southern Evangelicals. It kept them responsive to the common people, but it also enslaved their churches and institutions to the prejudices of the people. One conservative president of the Southern Baptist Convention phrased it well: "Democracy, such as Southern Baptists have, is like a log raft. You cannot guide the thing very well; you wallow all over the place; and your feet are always wet—but you can never sink a log raft. If you keep trying, you eventually get to a destination."[6]

Equally important was individualism. The notion that each person was responsible for his spiritual welfare fitted perfectly into a society renowned for its independence. One southern woman caught the spirit of southern folk religion perfectly in a legendary dictum: "What I am, I am, and nobody can't make me no ammer."

The centrality of conversion is apparent in the hymnology, organizational structure, and priorities of southern Evangelicals. Seldom

---

[5]For discussions of what makes southern Evangelicals unique, I relied on many sources. For comparisons of southern and northern Evangelicals, see Martin E. Marty, *Righteous Empire: The Protestant Experience in America* (New York: Dial Press, 1970), especially pp. 58-66. The best description of the homogeneous ideology of Presbyterians, Baptists, and Methodists which justifies the term "the Southern Church" is still Samuel S. Hill, Jr., *Southern Churches in Crisis* (Boston: Beacon Press, 1968). Several works are especially useful for the early stages of southern folk religion: Steve McNeely, "Early Baptists in the South, the Formation of a 'Folk Religion'," *The Quarterly Review* 35 (October-November-December 1974): 65-72; George Pullen Jackson, "Some Factors in the Diffusion of American Religious Folksongs," *Journal of American Folklore* 65 (October-December 1952): 365-69; Dickson D. Bruce, Jr., *And They All Sang Hallelujah: Plain Folk Camp-Meeting Religion, 1800-1845* (Knoxville: University of Tennessee Press, 1974); John B. Boles, *The Great Revival, 1787-1805* (Lexington: University of Kentucky Press, 1972); and Donald G. Mathews, *Religion in the Old South* (Chicago: University of Chicago Press, 1977).

[6]J. D. Grey, "Debate, Discussion for Decision, Not Division," *Baptist History and Heritage* 12 (October 1977): 231.

in the history of Christianity have so few people produced so many home and foreign missionaries or devoted so much of their material wealth to convert others. Although southern Evangelicals would cringe at the comparison, perhaps only the Jesuits brought such zeal to their tasks. This unity on the central religious issue is the force which held urban and rural, conservative, moderate, and liberal Evangelicals together. They could slay each other with Biblical quotations on race, evolution, the millennium and women deacons, then reunite on behalf of world evangelical outreach. This denominational loyalty, grounded in the imperative of evangelism, also made them cautious about the Fundamentalist Movement which historically insisted that loyalty to creed was more important than loyalty to denomination.[7] Although southern Evangelicals generally adopted fundamentalist theological positions, they were not prominent in the Fundamentalist Movement until the 1920s. Even then the most caustic Fundamentalists spent more time attacking other southern Evangelicals than anyone else and quickly lost influence in their own denominations. J. Frank Norris, the most famous Southern Baptist example, lost his influence in Texas and led his church out of the convention.

Although I would concede that emotion played a major role in southern folk religion, historians and sociologists have made too much of this. Not all practitioners of the religion of the head lived north of the Chesapeake, nor were all southern Evangelicals empty headed pew jumpers. Emotional religion earlier had found brilliant intellectual support in Jonathan Edwards and New England's New Light theologians. Conversely, Barton W. Stone, the father of the Cane Ridge revival of 1801 and himself a founder of the Disciples of Christ, regretted the emotional excesses of the great revivals. He argued his case in theology complicated and obtuse enough for even the most dogged systematizer.[8] In later years southern clergymen revised rational orthodox theology to serve the needs both of religious liberalism and conservatism.[9]

---

[7]Ernest R. Sandeen, *The Roots of Fundamentalism: British and American Millenarianism, 1800-1930* (Chicago: University of Chicago Press, 1970), pp. 73-75, 151-67, 240. Fundamentalist is used as an historic movement in western European theology which began in the reaction to the French Revolution.

[8]Hoke S. Dickinson, ed., *The Cane Ridge Reader* (n.p., 1972), especially pp. 6-247.

[9]Brooks Holifield, *The Gentlemen Theologians: American Theology in Southern Culture* (Durham: Duke University Press, 1978).

If emotion played a larger role for a longer time in southern folk religion than it did elsewhere, that is partly because the South remained a frontier longer than most sections, and as Richard Hofstadter brilliantly revealed some years ago, the frontier mind, whether religious or secular, tends to be anti-intellectual.

The South's preoccupation with original sin and guilt, in fact its altogether melancholy and pessimistic outlook on man, must be understood within the broader context of western man's post-Renaissance humanism. The rather grim medieval estimate of man gave way to an almost naive optimism about his potential by the time of the eighteenth century Enlightenment. Within this cycle of views, the religious pessimism which dominated southern folk religion seemed strangely out of step with American theology before 1939. But it does not seem so quaint since the advent of Neo-Orthodox theology. With Reinhold Niebuhr's post-1940 writings, especially *The Nature and Destiny of Man* (1941), *The Children of Light and the Children of Darkness* (1944), and *The Irony of American History* (1952), sin ceased to be a dirty three-letter word. Even psychology and psychiatry are not of one mind anymore (witness Karl Menninger's, *Whatever Became of Sin?*). What appeared as strangely regional theology before the 1940s has become at least acceptable, if not fashionable, perhaps yet another example of the southernization of America. Coupled with the rapid growth of fundamentalist religion in other regions since World War II, this exportation of southern evangelical thought demands far more attention than it has received.

What Functions Did Southern Evangelicalism Serve?

Focusing on the interaction of religious values and secular culture is only one way to examine the third question, the functions served by evangelical religion. Examining how Evangelicals sought to reform social and political injustices usually ends in a serious indictment of southern religion. Coming at religion from a more internal perspective—how it contributed to the Southerner's sense of self-worth, how it helped him make sense out of social reality, how it contributed to and helped maintain a sense of community—raises different questions and allows a more positive assessment.

The South's lack of originality in the classical art forms was balanced in part by its contributions to folk music, folk architecture, and folk art. I would add that the deficiencies of rational and systematic theology just catalogued should be weighed against the positive functions served by folk religion. Historian David Potter emphasized the fact that folk culture, with all its faults, provided a relatedness and meaning which urban industrial society was rapidly losing in the nineteenth century.[10] To be sure, ties of kinship and family are important in folk culture; as the saying goes, given time any two Southerners can establish kinship. But evangelical religion was the cement which held Southerners together despite the vagaries of time and history. Modern Americans are still wrestling with the question of how best to achieve a sense of belonging; but no one living in the age of the Peoples Temple, Moonies, Jesus Freaks, and a thousand communes and cults can seriously challenge the importance of a sense of community.

The conventional view of the southern church is that its overriding concern for personal conversion made Evangelicalism so individualistic that it had neither time nor interest for the community. True, up to a point. But equally important was its insistence on bringing the individual into intimate relationship with other people. A central function of the Great Revival between 1800 and 1815 was to substitute the order and discipline of Christian society for the disordered frontier world of violence and irresponsibility. Evangelicals rejected the emotional sterility and intellectual coldness of rational religion for a folk religion that emphasized social intimacy and mutual respect (offering the right hand of fellowship, love feasts, dinners on the ground, identifying terms such as "brother" and "sister," praying with arms around each other, greeting other Christians with a kiss, foot washing). Even church discipline had at its core the desire to help restore the chastized to a harmonious relationship with the Christian community.[11]

The organization into very small religious groups provided a tremendous source of strength in the face of trouble, and of troubles there seemed no end. An unhurried stroll through any nineteenth century graveyard impresses one with the mortality of man. A thousand inscriptions proclaim that "as for man, his life is like grass; he grows and flourishes like a wild flower. Then the wind blows on it, and it is gone, and no one sees it again":

---

[10]David M. Potter, *The South and the Sectional Conflict* (Baton Rouge: Louisiana State University Press, 1968), pp. 3-16.

[11]Mathews, *Religion in the Old South*, pp. 12, 39-46; Bruce, *They All Sang Hallelujah*, pp. 13-29, 114-15.

Theresa Scott
Darling Daughter of Theodore and Effie Scott
Born August 10, 1845 - Died January 15, 1847

David Jessup
Born July 12, 1872 - Died March 10, 1877

Add to the ephemerality of life, its drudgery, monotony, exhaustion and, for many, its poverty, and one has described the life experience of most nineteenth-century southern Evangelicals. Their goals and hopes were seldom realized. They had less than their fair share of money and power. So, conventional wisdom informs us, they retreated into an otherworldly, escapist religion. W. J. Cash describing the "Years the Cuckoo Claimed," 1914 to 1930, chronicled the rise of emotional religion, of traveling evangelists and faith healers. He wrote: "Beset with difficulties beyond his control and comprehension, increasingly taken in his vanity, puzzled, angered, frightened, the common white tended, like his fathers before him in the early days of the nineteenth century and in the Reconstruction time, to retreat into otherworldliness and, in the solace and the hope he found there, to resign himself to his lot in this world as of no more moment than a passing shadow cast in the sun by a cloud."[12]

In recent years both Jewish and Christian scholars have attempted to make Biblical sense out of "the reality we live in." Historically, a major function of both religions has been to help people understand social reality. In Europe the sense of being a people depended heavily on religious identification. When the immigrants came to America, their religion was the cement which bound ethnic communities together.[13]

In much the same way, their brand of Evangelicalism provided the ethnic Southerner a coherent view of his place in the world. A major theme of camp meeting hymns was the assurance of salvation, in contrast to preaching and exhorting which emphasized man's lostness. Conversion, the central theme of Evangelicals, brought a new world-view. Anticipation of the glories of heaven replaced the hopelessness of

---

[12]W. J. Cash, *The Mind of the South* (New York: Vintage Books, 1960), p. 297.

[13]Timothy L. Smith, "Religion and Ethnicity in America," *The American Historical Review* 83 (December 1978): 1155-85. Not all Smith's hypotheses about the relation between religion and ethnicity fit southern Evangelicals; but enough of them fit to provide a fascinating comparison.

the present world. This "canaan language" provided a bond of fellowship between evangelical blacks and whites. Many common people of both races, for quite different reasons, viewed existing conditions as intolerable and hoped for a different world to be created by divine intervention.[14] Such religion can be called other-worldly and escapist; indeed, that is the way in which most scholars view it.

I prefer psychiatrist Robert Coles' view that religion, at least for the rural poor, is an inescapable part of human meaning; in that sense, it is never wholly escapist.[15] A sociological survey of white Tennessee tenant farmers during the late 1930s documented Coles' point. In time of trouble, tenants found a resource: "If He had not stood by me, I would not have lived through the trouble I have had." Asked what difference it would make in their lives if they became convinced that no loving God cared for them, one tenant replied: "I'd feel like I was lost." Another responded: "Wouldn't have any encouragement then sure enough. Would just end it up sometime."[16]

That southern Evangelicals left many tasks undone, I would not debate. But in the rush to discover what was wanting, one must not ignore the functions Evangelicalism served: the affirmation of personal worth; the ordering of a chaotic world; providing an explanation of social reality; and creation of a sense of community.

What Was the Relationship of Southern Evangelicalism to Southern Culture?

No subject demonstrates better the problems of understanding southern Evangelicals than their relationship to culture. It is axiomatic among intellectuals that religion is the servant of culture. One study of Southern Baptist social thought (incidentally, a study considered to be revisionist by church historians because the author actually discovered some Baptist social thought) was entitled *Churches in Cultural Captivity*.

The inability of southern religion to escape the confining pressures of culture is, of course, not unique to Southern Baptists or even southern Evangelicals. Witness, for instance, the bitter divisions among Northern Baptists during the 1920s over evolution or more recently between

---

[14]Bruce, *They All Sang Hallelujah*, pp. 100-104.

[15]Robert Coles, "God and the Rural Poor," *Psychology Today* 5 (January 1972): 31-41.

[16]Quoted in Frank D. Alexander, "Religion in a Rural Community of the South," *American Sociological Review* 6 (April 1941): 241-51.

liberal and conservative wings of the Missouri Synod Lutheran Church. Advocates of change always accuse their brothers of being culture bound. Yet, one has to admit the basic thesis of W. J. Cash, Sam Hill, Martin Marty, H. Shelton Smith, and many others, that southern Evangelicals have been more faithful to southern culture than they have been to the radical ethics of Christ.

This thesis becomes increasingly difficult to understand when one examines it within the context of cultural pluralism. Assuming that white Baptists in Jefferson County, Alabama, are the servants of culture, which subcultures are served by Church of the Covenant, Berney Points, Vestavia Hills, Mountain Brook, Beverly and Powderly Baptist Churches? These churches obviously appeal to quite different classes, espouse different theologies, and serve different social needs. Some of them serve aspiring lower middle class families who resent any threat to their mobility. Others represent upper middle class people who "have arrived," who oppose social change, belong to the Chamber of Commerce and voted for Republican James Martin for the United States Senate. Still others serve blue collar people who hold tenaciously to fundamental theology while belonging to labor unions and voting for Democrat Donald Stewart for the Senate. One of these churches caters to well educated, politically liberal people who prefer a religious climate of openness and questioning. All these are legitimate human needs which religion helps meet. Jimmy Carter's election demonstrated to many Americans the diversity and sophistication of Evangelicals. Church historian Martin Marty has said that Carter's election did as much to bring Southern Baptists into the mainstream of American Protestantism as John Kennedy's election in 1960 did for Catholics.

Southern Evangelicalism always has served several subcultures. Perhaps it has not served as many as religion in other regions, hence its appearance of homogeneity; but its social thought has always been more diverse than most church historians have realized.

The long-recognized barriers to political action—excessive individualism, otherworldliness, fear of secular corruption, the view that politics and the exercise of political power is inherently evil—did not keep southern Evangelicals from active involvement in politics. They never adopted the repudiationist stance which called for the Christian to reject the secular world. The royal governor of North Carolina in the 1770s blamed rebellious Separate Baptists for the Regulator Movement. To the north, in Culpepper County, Virginia, Anglican officials arrested

Baptist preacher James Ireland for preaching his "vile, pernicious, abhorrent, detestable, abominable, diabolical doctrines." It is no surprise, then, to discover that southern Evangelicals constituted the core of support for the American Revolution in the otherwise Tory South. As a consequence of their political involvements, they emerged from the war with enhanced respect and considerable support among the South's common folk.[17] In the years which followed the Revolution, Evangelicals played a major role in the establishment of religious freedom in state constitutions, the growth of education and temperance reforms, and the defence of slavery, perhaps the preeminent political issue of the times.[18]

Such involvements have been acknowledged, but they constitute only a small portion of the story. I want to emphasize two more crucial areas of interaction between southern white Evangelicals and their culture, both having to do with the quality of rural and urban life.

One key to understanding the Evangelical's reaction to his culture is bivocationalism. Many ordained evangelical ministers did not earn their livelihood preaching. They worked full or part-time secular jobs and preached in addition to that. In 1976, for instance, 27 percent of all Southern Baptist churches were pastored by men employed in secular jobs. In churches of less than 300 members, 51 percent of the pastors were bivocational. Among music ministers serving the 35,000 Southern Baptist churches in 1978, 24,000 were part-time or voluntary workers, earning their livelihood elsewhere.[19] Bivocational ministers quite literally lived in two worlds, including a secular one which subjected them to the same frustrations, exploitations, and insecurity as their parishioners.

Perhaps the most obvious example of bivocationalism occurred in the rural South where it greatly influenced the way in which rural ministers viewed society. Presumably no more conservative American ever lived than the individualistic, rural, southern Evangelical. What always puzzled me about that assumption was that counties which were

---

[17]Richard A. McLemore, "Tumult, Violence, Revolution and Migration," *Baptist History and Heritage* 9 (October 1974): 230-36.

[18]See, for instance, Spencer Bidwell King, Jr., "Baptist Leaders in Early Georgia Politics," *The Quarterly Review* 38 (October-November-December 1977): 76-79; David Nelson Duke, "Henry Holcombe Tucker, Outspoken Baptist Journalist," *The Quarterly Review* 38 (October-November-December 1977):67-76.

[19]*Home Missions* 48 (October 1977): 5; *The Alabama Baptist,* July 27, 1978.

made up of precisely this kind of person staged the Populist revolt of the nineteenth century. Most of those who have tried to explain this contradiction have examined the wrong evidence. If one surveys the state denominational newspapers, for instance, he does not learn what all Evangelicals thought about Populists. Instead, he learns what Baptist or Methodist entrepreneurs who usually ran privately owned, run-for-profit newspapers thought. If he examines state or conference religious minutes and annual reports, he learns what the best educated pastors of the most prominent and wealthy churches thought.[20] Based on such evidence, one might think that only rural atheists voted the Populist ticket.

Let me balance this elitist approach to Evangelicals by suggesting what was happening among Alabama's common folk at the fork of the creek in the 1890s. Many evangelical farmer-pastors concluded that the only economic salvation for themselves and their parishioners was some form of government help. Since ministers possessed both community respect and oratorical skills, they became the natural leaders of the Populist cause. In Alabama, Baptist pastor Samuel M. Adams served as president of the state Farmers' Alliance, as head of the Populist Party, and was elected to a term in the state legislature. A conservative newspaper reporter heard the Baptist preacher address a farmer's institute in 1891 and commented:

> Mr. Adams is an easy and fluent speaker, but if he had stuck to his text we think it would have been more in accord of our idea of a Farmer's Institute. He is so full of politics that it was a hard matter for him to keep in the road.[21]

When chastized by fellow ministers for his political forays, Adams replied that "many of our brethren do not understand the true condition of the country" or they would be more concerned with the economic

---

[20]The best example of this kind of elitist analysis is Frederick A. Bode's *Protestantism and the New South: North Carolina Baptists and Methodists in Political Crisis, 1894-1903* (Charlottesville: University of Virginia Press, 1975). An excellent corrective to this view in Robert C. McMath, Jr., *Populist Vanguard: A History of the Southern Farmers' Alliance* (Chapel Hill: University of North Carolina Press, 1975). McMath writes that the idiom of agrarian protest was the language of evangelical Protestantism. Evangelical religion, concludes McMath, was as capable of supporting agrarian radicalism as of defending an unjust social order.

[21]Carrollton *West Alabamian*, July 1, 1891.

injustice in America.[22] Adams was closer to the feelings of the evangelical small farmer in the state than the editor of the state's Baptist paper. The editor of *The Alabama Baptist* had little sympathy for Populists and worried constantly about reports of unrest in the churches. Many Baptist pastors had "gone wild over politics." Laymen were so engrossed over secular issues that "they talked politics during Sunday School and outside the church, not coming into worship until after the prayer and Scripture reading." So bitter had the 1892 elections been that the editor of *The Alabama Baptist* warned that churches had been disturbed and "Christ's work neglected at many points." A country preacher wrote that his members became absorbed in politics, bad feelings were engendered, and a general coldness prevailed. The pastor of a church in rural eastern Alabama complained that his parishioners had more politics than religion. The pastor of Shiloh Church in Pike County wrote in 1893 that "the dreadful political excitement of last year had almost torn the church to pieces." A state Baptist leader returned from a mission tour of Alabama and used almost exactly the same words: "Many of our churches are torn to pieces on account of last year's politics." Methodist pastor W. M. McIntosh of Pickens County told his congregation in 1893 that the political strife of the previous year had been a greater curse to the churches than even "the whiskey traffic."[23] Baptist leaders, trying to explain why an unprecedented number of their pastors were running for public office, noted that many of them were impoverished farmers.[24] Obviously something was amiss in the rural Zion.

The quality of rural life improved only marginally after the turn of the century. By 1916 half the rural churches in America were in the South and within those churches bivocational ministers labored. Many of them pastored more than one church; some of them pastored as many as four or five. Many of these marginal churches had no educational program and no organizations for women or children. Of the total 44,300 white Baptist and Methodist churches in the South in 1916, 82 percent were rural; and of these, 90 percent had preaching only once a month. Some 80 percent of these rural churches were served by absentee pastors. Of 3,430 Presbyterian churches in the South in 1913, 271 had no pastors.[25] Nor did

---

[22]*The Alabama Baptist*, March 24, 1892.

[23]Ibid., July 21 and 28, 1892; December 10, 1891; July 5, 1894; August 10 and 24, 1893.

[24]Ibid., January 7 and July 21, 1892.

[25]Victor I. Masters, *Country Church in the South* (Atlanta: Home Mission Board, 1916), p. 119.

conditions improve markedly until after World War II. As late as 1947 there were still 1,946 Baptist churches in Alabama which met irregularly, and 1,600 Baptist churches which relied on bivocational preachers.

Statistics do not capture the depth of deprivation of many southern Evangelicals. In the mountains of southwestern Virginia in 1915 one untrained Baptist minister pastored two churches for a year. He spent three weeks in revivals and earned a total salary of $13.20. With his family, he lived in a two-room cabin on thirty acres of rented land. He worked for a neighbor part-time in exchange for a horse to plow his corn field. On alternate Sundays he walked to his churches, one of which was six miles away, the other five. In the same region another pastor worked at a grist mill all week and earned an annual salary from his churches of less than thirty dollars.[26] Dr. J. W. Lester, Alabama's rural minister of the year in 1949, began preaching full-time in 1932 in four rural churches near Alexander City. Eagle Creek Baptist Church paid him $36.47 for the year; the salary at Rockie Creek was $33.00; New Salem paid him nothing; and Elam paid $215.66; a total of $285.23 for the year.[27]

Such conditions spawned two reactions. First, some denominational leaders developed greater interest in the quality of rural life.[28] Denominational colleges began to offer courses in rural sociology. The 1913 meeting of the Southern Baptist Home Mission Board created a special rural ministry called the Department of Enlistment (the title is important; when Evangelicals tried to reform society it was imperative that it be done in the name of evangelical outreach). This agency employed fifteen ministers to work with rural Baptist associations to try to reduce farm tenancy, improve the quality of home and farm life for rural southern women, reform farming practices, encourage the formation of rural organizations that would reduce the isolation, soften the individualism, and stimulate the social lives of rural people. Dr. Lester, one of the missionaries appointed under the new program, not only preached on original sin; other sermon titles included "The Relationship of Wise Land Use to the Churches, the Schools, the Homes,

---

[26]Ibid., p. 98.

[27]Dr. J. W. Lester Papers, Auburn University Archives.

[28]Masters, *Country Church*; Edmund des. Brunner, *Church Life in the Rural South* (N.Y.: George H. Doran Company, 1923); L. G. Wilson, et al., "The Church and Landless Men," University of North Carolina *Bulletin*, 1 (March 1, 1922): 1-27.

and Other Social Agencies," "And He Will Heal Their Land" (the damaging consequences of soil erosion), and "The Rural Church Faces the Future." He studied rural sociology, ultimately becoming so expert that he was asked to lecture at Baptist seminaries and at Auburn University. He showed films in his churches on sanitary methods of milking cows. After he retired from his rural pastorate in Alabama, he became head of the Rural Church Department at Clear Creek Baptist School in the mountains of eastern Kentucky where the average preacher-student was aged thirty and had a ninth grade education. He assigned them books on rural sociology including Arthur Raper's 1936 indictment of farm tenancy, *Preface to Peasantry*. While he taught the men, his wife traveled the remote hollows of Appalachia teaching six hundred mountain women the Laubach literacy program so that they could spread education among isolated and poverty-stricken mountain people.

The Methodist Bureau of Christian Social Relations began studying problems of the rural South as early as 1912. In 1930 the Woman's Missionary Council created the Committee on Rural Develoment which proposed an extensive program of community reforms to improve rural life in general and especially the plight of rural women.

A second reaction to rural blight was more in the Populist tradition. Particularly among angry Evangelicals in the Southwest, socialism thrived between 1910 and 1924. Socialist-minded evangelical ministers used camp meeting strategies and the religious idiom to transform secular socialism into a transcendant faith in universal brotherhood and economic justice. Clinging all the while to their individualistic culture traditions, they fought tenaciously against the domination of capitalistic large scale agriculture, urban values, and wealthy town churches.[29] To say that southern Evangelicals ignored the problems of rural America is not accurate, although they awakened to those problems more slowly than Evangelicals in other regions.

Interest in urban problems increased slowly among a people so overwhelmingly rural. Most Methodists and Baptists at the turn of the

[29]Garin Burbank, *When Farmers Voted Red: The Gospel of Socialism in the Oklahoma Countryside, 1910-1924* (Westport, Connecticut: Greenwood Press, 1976); and James R. Green, *Grass-Roots Socialism: Radical Movements in the Southwest, 1895-1943* (Baton Rouge: Louisiana State University Press, 1978), especially chapter four, "Propagating the Socialist Gospel," pp. 126-75.

century feared the city and believed it corrupted morals and loosened family ties. One Baptist leader captured the spirit of most Evangelicals when he wrote: "Men, like hogs, are bred in the country to be consumed in the towns."[30]

Among people directly affected by urbanization, attitudes began to change rapidly after 1900. Two dissimilar groups of Evangelicals contributed to urban reform. On one hand, there were denominational leaders well educated in national currents of thought. Many of them were influenced by the social Christianity becoming fashionable in the urban North and Midwest. The other group consisted of working class preachers, themselves coal miners or textile mill workers, who carried their class interests into the pulpit.

For decades historians denied the existence of the Social Gospel in the South, but recent research has demonstrated that scholars, like Evangelicals, do make mistakes.[31] As workers deserted the church because they believed it cared nothing for their problems, sensitive clerics in increasing numbers advocated change. Temperance was the preeminent reform of the era, and it was usually viewed as a matter of social and not private morality. Because prohibition demanded that Evangelicals enter politics, it produced a generation of shrewd, effective church lobbyists. Once involved in the political process, many Evangelicals enlarged their reform agenda.

The changes they proposed addressed almost all the major urban-industrial problems of the day. In Birmingham, for example, Dr. Henry

---

[30]Quoted in Masters, *Country Church*, p. 40.

[31]A sample of the newer scholarship which acknowledges the social conscience of southern Evangelicals includes: George B. Tindall, *The Emergence of the New South, 1913-1945* (Baton Rouge: Louisiana State University Press, 1967), especially pp. 196-200; Kenneth K. Bailey, *Southern White Protestantism in the Twentieth Century* (New York: Harper and Row, 1964); John Lee Eighmy, "Religious Liberalism in the South During the Progressive Era," *Church History* 38 (September 1969): 359-72; Wayne Flynt, "Dissent in Zion: Alabama Baptists and Social Issues, 1900-1914," *The Jornal of Southern History* 35 (November 1969): 523-42; Flynt, "Religion in the Urban South: The Divided Religious Mind of Birmingham, 1900-1930," *The Alabama Review* 30 (April 1977): 108-34; Flynt, "Alabama White Protestantism and Labor, 1900-1914," *The Alabama Review* 25 (July 1972): 192-217; Flynt, "Organized Labor, Reform, and Alabama Politics, 1920," *The Alabama Review* 23 (July 1970): 163-80; Billy Storms, "Southern Baptists and a Social Gospel: An Uneasy Alliance," unpublished seminar paper, Southern Baptist Theological Seminary, 1975, copy in author's possession.

M. Edmonds led the congregation of Independent Presbyterian Church into a broad Social Gospel program. His church, the result of a split within more fundamentalist South Highlands Presbyterian Church, helped organize the Jefferson County Children's Aid Society, hired a female member of the church staff to assist the jobless, a nurse to aid the poor, and a social worker for the Northside Community House; the church also constructed the Children's Fresh Air Farm which provided summertime nourishment and recreation for 8,000 poor white children between 1920 and 1950.

Women in the Methodist Episcopal Church, South, began a settlement house ministry in 1893. Situated in working class neighborhoods, the Wesley and Bethlehem Houses provided day schools where working women could leave children, night literacy programs for working boys, and free kindergartens. Such a house was opened in Birmingham in June, 1903. So successful was the initial effort, that additional houses were built behind Avondale mills and for Italian steelworkers at Ensley.

Methodists in Mobile began an even more ambitious program in 1904. By 1910 Mobile's Wesley House was called "the best all around social agency in the city." In addition to the services provided by the Birmingham settlement houses, the Mobile facility operated a free medical dispensary which took care of sick indigents without charge. In 1910 a staff of five doctors performed surgery at the house with scaled charges based on income.[32] By 1920 there were at least forty-four such Methodist settlement houses serving both races in the urban South.[33]

Baptists had more difficulty institutionalizing their social concerns. The editor of Alabama's denominational newspaper from 1901 until 1919 was Frank W. Barnett. Although a theological conservative, he edited a reform newspaper which treated nearly every social question of the time. On labor conditions in Birmingham, he wrote: "Churches have frequently shut their eyes to the struggles of labor to get a minimum wage; and have not heard the cry of the children who were being

---

[32]Careful attention to the *Methodist Alabama Christian Advocate* between 1900 and 1914 reveals hundreds of articles on the settlement houses and urban problems in general.

[33]Noreen Dunn Tatum, *A Crown of Service: A Story of Woman's Work in the Methodist Episcopal Church South, From 1878-1940* (Nashville: Parthenon Press, 1960), pp. 241-81.

sacrificed in our mills; or cared when a fight was being made for shorter hours and better working conditions." Next to temperance, the issue which he addressed most frequently during these years was child labor. He urged Baptists to write their legislative representatives and to join the Alabama Child Labor Committee; by such policies, he organized a powerful lobby. When the legislature postponed reform in 1907 he thundered: "Who keeps a lobby, day in and day out, watching these bills? Who appears at hearings, trying to have them defeated or amended in such a way that they fail? . . . The attorney of cotton manufacturers, of glass manufacturers, the paid representatives of the oppressors are there, but who represents you and me in our earnest desire to see justice done to the children?" When his plea fell on deaf ears, he wrote: "Let us call [child labor] by its right name—murder. But if the death comes quickly enough, it is less cruel than the life to which such boys and girls are condemned." Largely due to his efforts, the second session of the 1907 Alabama legislature passed a child labor bill that was called the "most effective child labor law that has thus far been enacted in the South."[34]

Middle class reformers risked very little with such proposals because they were also endorsed by progressive businessmen, teachers, lawyers, and even some southern politicians. On more "radical" questions such as collective bargaining, strikes, and socialism, Evangelicals were generally cautious. Many mill and mine owners were influential laymen who used religion as a method of social control. Liston Pope, in his classic study *Millhands and Preachers*, quoted an obituary from the *Gastonia* (North Carolina) *Gazette* describing a deceased mill owner: "He served his church and pastor well, and was a bulwark of safe conservatism and orthodox religion in all the church courts."[35] Such wealthy parishioners donated land for churches, paid for buildings, and subsidized ministers' salaries. Denominational leaders, in turn, were properly deferential, praised the civic mindedness of pious laymen, and opposed strikes.[36]

---

[34]See *The Alabama Baptist*, June 18, 1913; February 13, 1907; and November 15, 1973 (for Wayne Flynt's essay "The Cry of the Children").

[35]Quoted in Liston Pope, *Millhands and Preachers* (New Haven: Yale University Press, 1942), pp. 16-17.

[36]For instance, see Jonathan O. Beasley, "The Reaction of the Southern Baptist Press to the Haymarket Incident of 1866," *The Quarterly Review* 33 (January-February-March 1973): 37-42.

As in the Populist movement, however, the bivocational minister who labored in mine or mill often approached these problems quite differently. During a particularly violent 1914 strike in the West Virginia coal fields, miners held a meeting in Wellsburg. The mixture of native born whites and immigrant miners from Italy and eastern Europe applauded incendiary speeches denouncing capitalism. *The Wheeling Majority* (West Virginia) ended its account of the rally with a matter-of-fact sentence: "After Mr. Levinski [a national organizer for the U.M.W.] had spoken in their own language to the Slavish and Polish, the audience was requested to turn out in a body that night and attend the revival service at the Tabernacle now being conducted in Wellsburg."

Six years later, in 1920, miners struck the Red Jacket Coal Company in Mingo County, West Virginia. In May of that year 500 miners held a rally in Matewan. A preacher named Combs "made a radical talk" denouncing the company. Urging miners to refuse to sign contracts with the company, Combs said that any miner who signed it was "not as good as a yellow dog." Any superintendent who would ask a fellow human to sign such an agreement "carried a gizzard around in a heart's place."

When West Virginia's labor dispute degenerated into a bloody war in 1922, the man who led the miners was Reverend John Wilburn, who had pastored the Baptist Church in Blair, West Virginia, since 1915. To supplement his preacher's salary he mined coal side by side with his parishioners. An organizational genius who did not confine his talent to the Sunday School, Wilburn established armed patrols which gained control of Blair Mountain and the passes leading to it. At one briefing he harangued his troops, suggesting that they lay siege to the town of Logan and that they take no prisoners. Intercepted on the march to Logan by sheriff's deputies, the miners fought a pitched battle that resulted in deaths on both sides. Before the affair ended, the United States Army was sent to the area and the air force conducted a bombing raid on Blair Mountain to dislodge the parson and his troops. John Wilburn was tried for treason and other charges, convicted of murder, but later pardoned.[37]

Such events were not as rare as the scarcity of written records indicate. Oral histories are only now giving such poorly educated Evangelicals a voice, and what we are hearing does not coincide with long

---

[37]Richard D. Lunt, *Law and Order vs. the Miners: West Virginia, 1907-1933* (Hamden, CT: Archon Books, 1979), pp. 43, 134-35, 162.

accepted stereotypes. One Baptist minister in Greensboro, North Carolina, left a powerful narrative of the 1930s. He had entered the textile mill to work at age fifteen and had progressed well before "surrendering" to the call to preach. He praised the company for its support of churches and preachers' salaries (his church paid a generous salary of $2,060 a year). When the workers organized in the 1920s and went on strike, he tried not to take sides ("our work not bein' mill work but the salvation of souls"). But as parishioners came to him to express their grievances, he began to change his mind, finally concluding that southern textile workers ought to organize. He looked to Washington for help, and his congregation sent him to Roosevelt's 1932 inauguration. He reported his impressions to the church when he returned:

> But as I stood there in that vast throng watchin' Hoover
> go out and Mr. and Mrs. Roosevelt come in, I felt like weepin'.
> I thought, one man of big promise goes out and another comes
> in, and like always the people go on in need. When the people
> is helped, it'll be when they've waked up to their rights.[38]

Even if such memories are flawed by time and are sometimes self-serving, they do suggest another dimension of the southern evangelical mind.

Who were mainstream southern Evangelicals? A mixture of rural farmers and urban workers and businessmen, rich and poor. What did they believe? Essentially they were individualistic and felt more comfortable with a religion that consoled the heart than with one that troubled the mind. The function of their religion? To help them understand the world they lived in, to comfort them in times of trouble, to provide a sense of personal worth. Southern Evangelicalism's relation to culture? Diverse, depending on class and time and needs. Whatever the southern mind was, we will never comprehend it until we understand southern religion.

---

[38]Tom E. Terrill and Jerrold Hirsch, *Such As Us: Southern Voices of the Thirties* (Chapel Hill: University of North Carolina Press, 1978), pp. 167-68. This entire oral history, entitled "There's Always a Judas," and the following one, "When a Man Believes," reveal the depth of social protest among evangelical textile workers.

The South:
Seedbed of Sectarianism

David Edwin Harrell, Jr.

In the minds of most Americans the twentieth century South remains a curious mixture of earnest, toothy Evangelicals and briar-hopping, Bible-thumping, snake-handling zealots. The two images often run together to form a stereotype Fundamentalist. In a moment of anger at the Scopes trial, Clarence Darrow admitted that he had come to Dayton to save the South from "bigots and ignoramuses," by which he meant William Jennings Bryan and the leading citizens of Dayton, Tennessee. H. L. Mencken, astonished by the whole Dayton affair, pronounced the South a religious funny farm where prohibition was essential lest the drunken farmers let their milk cows burst and few of his readers then or now have questioned his judgment. This Bible Belt formula, true as it was in many ways, obscured the interesting and important diversity of the religion of the South.

Southern mainstream religious leaders were never quite so uniformly backward and anti-intellectual as Mencken imagined. Southern Evangelicals, or, to use the more pejorative term, Fundamentalists, could easily be taken as bigots, but, from another perspective, they were simply the keepers of the old order fighting for the survival of the Christian system against the powerful onslaught of authoritarian science and secularism. They fought with the tools they had at hand, sometimes with emotional and anti-intellectual tirades and sometimes with logic and studied scientific and theological rebuttals. Their stance against Darwinism and other new ideas was sensible to them and, despite the judgment of one recent historian that "defeats suffered by the Fundamentalists in the 1920s insured that few Protestants would ever again call themselves Fundamentalists,"[1] it is a war that has by no means ended. Jerry Falwell, independent Baptist pastor in Lynchburg, Virginia, proudly wore the name "Fundamentalist" and presided over a sixty million dollar a year religious empire in 1980; an impressed Ronald Reagan confessed that he believed the theory of evolution was still unproven. While in the White House Jimmy Carter read his Bible every day, "witnessed" to visiting heads of state, and in all probability swallowed the story of Jonah and the whale.

Beneath this lively and little understood troop of Fundamentalists lies yet another layer of southern religion, a numerous and persistent group who look upon Fundamentalists as compromisers and on Southern Baptists as liberals. The twentieth century South was a seedbed for radical Christian sects with all their characteristic traits, otherworldly hope, an antagonistic relationship with the world, aberrant social behavior, and ardent evangelical zeal. Clarence Darrow's colleague at Dayton, the urbane Arthur Garfield Hays, listened in stunned silence as a group of "Holy Rollers" shouted: "Thank God I got no education. Glory be to God."[2] While some Fundamentalists shared this low estimate of education, most protested only against "science, falsely so called." Hays had caught a glimpse of the radical sectarian religion of the South's poor whites, of southern religious populism. Southern religion might appear monolithic when faced with the threat of Darwinism, but when the excitement abated, the "Holy Rollers" would have urged William Jennings Bryan to pray on through and seek the baptism of the Spirit. In the first half of the twentieth century the South was covered by that virulent strain of Christians who believed the way was narrow indeed and who doubted the eternal salvation of their most devout neighbors.

---

[1] *Student's Guide to the Long Search: A Study of Religions* (Dubuque, Iowa: Kendall/Hunt Publishing Company, 1978), p. 197.

[2] Quoted in Willard B. Gatewood, Jr., ed., *Controversy in the Twenties* (Nashville: Vanderbilt University Press, 1969), p. 333.

It had not always been so. In the nineteenth century religious radicalism flourished mostly in other sections of the nation. The great revivals of the pre-Civil War period were primarily western and northern and the most important new nineteenth-century sects, the Disciples of Christ, Mormons, adventists, and holiness, were clearly products of those regions. Southerners were proud that their religion had remained more traditional. In 1833, one southern minister boasted: "Mormonism, adventism, sanctificationism, spiritualism, women's rights, free love, and all such, started north of Mason and Dixon's line."[3]

The South's avoidance of sectarianism in the nineteenth century high-lighted the region's religious uniformity in the midst of a century of change. Southerners remained Bible-believing rationalists, the heirs of a reformed tradition which was essentially conservative, rationalistic, millennialistic and common-sensical.[4] Southern churchmen entered the twentieth century as the stalwart defenders of the old order; many southern Evangelicals still read nineteenth-century books and have nineteenth-century minds. A Nashville preacher wrote in 1891: "The Southern Methodists are protesting against the tendency to reject the word of God by the Northern Methodists. Southern Presbyterians are objecting to the loose teachings of their Northern brethren. Baptists South are protesting against setting aside the word of God by their Northern brethren, and loose rationalistic and semi-infidel teachings are prevailing in some churches of Disciples in the Northern states."[5] In 1925, in the aftermath of the Scopes Trial, a southern magazine boasted that the incident would be "one of the South's supremist advertisements." "There are millions of people in other parts of the United States," the editor wrote, "who do not want to raise their children in an atmosphere of agnosticism and atheism so prevalent throughout the North and West, where the alien foreign element is so dominant, and who, having learned as a result of this trial that there is a section in this country where religion pure and undefiled still holds sway, will turn their

---

[3] James L. Thornberry, "The North East Iowa Christian Association," *Gospel Advocate* 25 (February 8, 1883): 89.

[4] Two recent books which make this point are Theodore Dwight Bozeman, *Protestants in an Age of Science* (Chapel Hill: University of North Carolina Press, 1977); and Fred J. Hood, *Reformed America* (University, Alabama: The University of Alabama Press, 1980).

[5] "Should Women Preach Publicly," *Gospel Advocate* 33 (August 5, 1891): 486.

eyes longingly to the land of Promise, hoping that in the South they may be able to have their children raised in an atmosphere of Christianity."[6] The choices were limited, wrote an Arkansas Baptist preacher in 1919, since "the bulk of the Democracy of the United States" was made up of "the Baptist South and the riff-raff Roman Catholic elements of the North."[7]

In spite of this seemingly solid front, southern religion began to fragment at the turn of the century. Scores of new churches were born in the early twentieth century, all militantly protesting against the mainstream southern churches. The two most important sectarian streams to appear—the birth year of each is sometimes associated with the religious census of 1906—were the Churches of Christ and Pentecostalism. The Churches of Christ has been a relatively more unified movement, although in the first half of the twentieth century the group suffered divisions over premillennialism, the use of multiple containers in communion, Sunday schools, the use of head coverings by women and various moral issues such as divorce, modest dress, and Christian participation in the military or other government service. Pentecostalism's development was even more chaotic. Scores of new churches were born in the twenty years after 1900. The Assemblies of God, the Church of God, and the Pentecostal Holiness Church were the largest, but the list included Triumph the Church and Kingdom of God in Christ, the Pillar of Fire Church, and the United Holy Church of North Carolina and Virginia. One Pentecostal leader described the disorder of the period: "They began to have divisions, splits and controversies. Soon they began to split their splits. Nearly every church was either a split or a splinter."[8] Pentecostals divided over countless doctrinal issues, including a major and bitter dispute over trinitarianism, and were riddled by personality clashes. Add to these two movements the persistent independence of many Baptist churches and the South was clearly the most fertile source of sectarianism in the United States in the first half of the twentieth century.

These new churches were vital and successful as well as

---

[6]Quoted in Gatewood, *Controversy in the Twenties*, p. 354.

[7]"Strange Bed Fellows," *Baptist Advance* 18 (January 30, 1919): 4.

[8]David Nunn and W. V. Grant, *The Coming World-Wide Revival* (Dallas: W. V. Grant, n.d.), p. 23.

characteristically sectarian. The Churches of Christ and the larger Pentecostal churches were the fastest growing religious groups in the nation for several decades. While all of the new churches had congregations throughout the country, the Churches of Christ were strongest in Tennessee, North Alabama, and Texas; the Assemblies of God in Missouri, Arkansas, Oklahoma, and Texas; the Church of God in Tennessee, the Carolinas, and Georgia; and the Pentecostal Holiness Church in Georgia and Oklahoma.[9]

Few middle-class Americans in North or South took the new sects seriously in their early years and the sects intentionally isolated themselves from the mainstream southern churches. For instance, the sects had little to do with the raging Fundamentalist-Modernist controversy in the 1920s. At best, they were mildly supportive of the fundamentalist warriors. But mostly they went their independent ways. The Churches of Christ disdained cooperation with "outsiders," regarding all other churches as "apostates" and "false religionists."[10] Many Pentecostals were equally exclusive and even the most irenic, who expressed some interest in joining the organized Fundamentalist movement, were regarded as so disreputable by mainstream Evangelicals that their overtures were rejected.

The proliferation of sects in the South after the turn of the century bears no simple explanation. Clearly, slavery and the loss of the Civil War pushed the South toward otherworldly and legalistic religious views. Southerners found support for slavery in literalistic readings of the Bible, while Northerners argued much more generally that the principle of love excluded social injustice. Northern Christians emerged from the Civil War confident that their cause had been holy and filled with a new secular optimism. On the other hand, southern Christians were humbled by defeat and took refuge in submission to God's will and trust in His otherworldly promises. In short, slavery and defeat pushed southern

---

[9]See Wilbur Zelinsky, "An Approach to the Religious Geography of the United States: Patterns of Church Membership in 1952," *Annals* of the American Association of Geographers 51 (June, 1961): 139-91; and Edwin Scott Gaustad, *Historical Atlas of Religion in America* (New York: Harper & Row, Publishers, 1962), pp. 121-26.

[10]See Earl Irvin West, *The Search for the Ancient Order*, 2 vols. (Nashville: Gospel Advocate Co., 1953).

religion toward classical sectarian views. Such thinking made the South fertile soil for a sectarian revival, but, in the years immediately after the war, the mainstream evangelical churches were so theologically conservative that no new sects were born. Ostracized and defeated, southern white churches, like southern society, were uniformly conservative for a generation. The sectarian outbreak at the turn of the century, which roughly paralleled the populist movement, was a conscious rebellion by the South's poorest whites.

The rise of the sectarian South also was related to the violent disruption of southern society in the late nineteenth and twentieth centuries. Religious historians have convincingly tied the sectarian religion of early nineteenth century America to the breakup of traditional New England society. In the late nineteenth-century South changes in race relations, new agricultural patterns and the beginnings of urbanization and industrialization uprooted and bewildered many Southerners. Large numbers of southern farmers not only became tenants, they also became migrants, placing great pressure on the traditional family structure.[11] Clearly, these social changes threatened Southerners more directly than a wide acceptance of new ideas in the region. This social stress produced in the South, as it had in other societies, two contradictory themes—a frantic, almost paranoid, reassertion of old values and an instability which bred religious hysteria and experimentation. The result was a hothouse for sects.

The most tangible single explanation for the southern sectarian revival, however, was poverty—the grinding, pervasive, unrelenting poverty of millions of white Southerners between the Civil War and World War II. Deprivation has always been the breeding ground for religious zealots. That the new sects of the South ministered to the needs of the desperately poor is made clear in the religious census reports of the early twentieth century. In 1936 the average value of the property of an urban New England church was over $75,000; the figure for southern churches was about $22,000; in the state of Mississippi it was $11,611. A large percentage of southern churches were rural and here the figures

---

[11]See Katherine A. Cullen, "The Decline of Prosperity in Pleasant Ridge: A Look at a Beat in Greene County, Alabama, 1860-1870" (unpublished manuscript in the possession of the author). Ms. Cullen, along with several other doctoral students at the University of Alabama, has been studying mobility in the late nineteenth century South through a detailed analysis of names in the census.

were even starker. The average value of the church property of a rural New England church was $17,166; in the South it was $3,200.[12]

The relative poverty of all southern churches was only a part of the story. There were great variations within the region. For instance, the average value of the property of a Southern Baptist church was a relatively respectable $9,500. The figure declined rapidly as one moved from the larger to the smaller sects: the Churches of Christ, about $3,500; the Assemblies of God, slightly over $3,300; the Tomlinson Church of God (later the Church of God of Prophecy), a little over $1,800; and the Church of God, less than $1,500. The average value of the property held by a Church of God in Mississippi in 1936 was $474.[13]

The poor's churches have long been the best, and sometimes the only, mirror of their minds, being the only institution under their control. The importance of the black church in southern society finds its parallel in southern poor white sects. In each case the church spoke the mind of a powerless minority and survived precisely for that reason. When one listens to the sectarians of the first half of the twentieth century—hearing beyond the sometimes bizarre doctrinal pronouncements that form the theological bases for their existence—one hears an atypical and unexpected variation of southern thought.

Particularly in their formative stages, sects frequently espouse variant social views, as well as unusual doctrinal positions. Sometimes these views grow out of novel theological interpretations carried to logical extremes, but more often they simply reflect the willingness of the dispossessed to experiment with the dominant mores of the society.

For instance, the most dramatic religious departures from the southern racist gospel after the Civil War came in the sectarian community. In 1878, David Lipscomb, an austere, farm-bred Church of Christ editor from Nashville, wrote: "For our part, we would much prefer membership with an humble and despised band of ignorant negroes, than with a congregation of the aristocratic and refined whites of the land." "The church was established," he continued, "to help the lowly, the fallen . . . the outcast and the degraded."[14] In the 1880s pioneer

---

[12]Bureau of the Census, *Religious Bodies: 1936,* 2 vols. (Washington: United States Government Printing Office, 1941), 1:166.

[13]Ibid., 2:1:68, 120, 404, 429, 466.

[14]"Race Prejudice," *Gospel Advocate* 20 (February 21, 1878):121.

Pentecostal evangelist Mrs. Woodworth-Etter conducted integrated revivals in the South, as did Aimee Semple McPherson in the 1920s.[15] Southern Pentecostalism was unusually color blind throughout the early twentieth century.

This legacy carried over into the post-World War II period when the poor people's sects and a coterie of independent evangelists consistently challenged racial segregation. The first cases of racial integration in southern religion came not in the liberal churches that fought bitter battles in the late 1960s and 1970s, but in the small sects. Many of the early Pentecostal denominations began as interracial churches, and although most of the larger ones later segregated, some of the smaller sects continued to include members of both races. In 1965 the magazine of the Church of God of Prophecy defended its integrated General Assembly: "To have racial distinction would be against the will of God or the purpose of the Church. . . . The speckled bird has many different colored feathers, and so is the Church of the last days. . . . I feel like shouting when I think of the oneness that is to be found in Christ Jesus."[16]

The Church of God of Prophecy was only the moderate tip of this unexposed layer of southern religion and society. By the mid-1960s the group was forty years old and was a well-developed sect. While its general assemblies were integrated all of its local churches were segregated. Farther out on the sectarian frontier were scores of newer groups, many of them bolder in their racial conduct. The Church of God (Jerusalem Acres), born in the late 1940s, was fully integrated. In 1966, the chief bishop of the church strongly supported the civil rights movement in a sermon at the church's headquarters in Cleveland, Tennessee, squarely in the midst of a poor white neighborhood in a small mountain village: "Yes, I state again the only difference between a Negro and a white is his skin, and he who fights to keep the land free should enjoy the freedom of the land. He pays taxes, so why should he be forbidden to vote just because he cannot read or write? The reason most southern Negroes cannot read and write is because there were no schools prepared for

---

[15]See M. B. Woodworth-Etter, *Marvels and Miracles* (Indianapolis: Mrs. M. B. Woodworth-Etter, 1927), pp. 57-59; Nancy Barr Mavity, *Sister Aimee* (New York: Doubleday, Doran & Company, 1931), p. 38.

[16]E. A. Crossfield, "The Church is Not Subject to Racial or National Frontiers," *White Wing Messenger* 42 (June 5, 1965): 6.

them. I know the move the Negro leaders are now making is of God. The prayers of our colored people have come up before God, and He is going to release His colored people. Christ died for all colors."[17] When Martin Luther King, Jr. was assassinated, the chief bishop urged his followers to embrace the cause of blacks: "Dr. King fought for the freedom and recognition of his people. One cannot be a true Christian ... and yet have a feeling that the colored man is inferior to him. When a man is not allowed to eat in a restaurant, drink at a water fountain, use rest room facilities, or ride in a certain part of any public transportation because of the color of his skin, you may rest assured that this is a measure of slavery and partiality with which God is not pleased."[18]

Even bolder was the racial behavior of the band of roving tent evangelists who crisscrossed the South in the years after World War II as the forerunners of the modern charismatic revival.[19] Beginning in the early 1950s these revivalists ministered to both blacks and whites. Their audiences included the most economically and religiously deprived part of southern society. In the early 1950s, their meetings were segregated into black and white sections, but by the later part of the decade that pattern had begun to change. The most extreme evangelists, those who appealed to independent Pentecostals and the poorest people, increasingly turned to blacks for support. They also increasingly erased the color line.

The most influential of the healing evangelists working in the South in the 1950s and 1960s was A. A. Allen. Allen conducted integrated revivals in the South as early as 1952 but said little about the race issue. But by the end of the 1950s Allen began to emphasize the biracial character of his ministry. He was especially proud of breaking the racial barrier in southern cities such as Atlanta, Little Rock, and Winston-Salem. In 1958, after a campaign in Little Rock, Allen's promotional magazine, *Miracle Magazine*, reported: "When hearts are hungry and

---

[17]"Integration and the Bible," (Mimeographed sermon; October, 1966), pp. 4-5.

[18]"The Shot Heard Around the World," *The Vision Speaks* 11 (May, 1968): 4.

[19]See David Edwin Harrell, Jr., *White Sects and Black Men in the Recent South* (Nashville: Vanderbilt University Press, 1971). Will Campbell tells an interesting story about a Church of God preacher in his *Brother to a Dragonfly* (New York: Seabury Press, 1977), pp. 156-59.

God is moving, there is no time for color lines!"[20] During the 1960s, when mainstream southern churches were wrestling with troubled consciences in all-white congregations, the big tents of the healing revivalists moved through every city of the South hosting tens of thousands of blacks and whites who found on their benches a common haven from their wretched poverty.

Nor was race an isolated issue. Poor white religion was less bound by social convention in other areas. After the violent national strikes of the 1890s, a caustic Church of Christ preacher-debater, J. D. Tant, offhandedly asked: "If organized capital can put guns into the hands of their subjects to shoot down those who will not submit to their rule, why may not labor arm itself for protection?"[21] In his classic study of labor organizing in the textile mills in North Carolina, Liston Pope discovered that the only religious leaders who consistently supported the workers were the preachers of the small sects.[22] Indeed, the only southern religious leaders to consistently challenge the dominant social values of the section in the twentieth century have been the prophets of the poor.

Were southern sectarians then social and political revolutionaries? Quite to the contrary. Most were almost totally disinterested in social reform and some were theologically opposed to political action. The social nonconformity of southern sects was individualistic and independent, but never rebellious. The abjectly and permanently poor no longer cared whether others approved of their actions. They did what they perceived to be right, and what came naturally (for instance, associating with blacks and sympathizing with labor), because they had no status to lose. Having no hope of changing society, they placed within a religious context the most obvious truths their experience taught them.

The heart of the sectarian gospel, however, and the key to its appeal to the southern poor after 1900, was a three-pronged message which gave spiritual meaning to poverty, offered an otherworldly escape, and held out a slim hope for miraculous relief from suffering. These escapist and narcotic ideas made sense to destitute Southerners.

---

[20] "Miracle in Black and White," *Miracle Magazine* 3 (August, 1958): 10. See Howard Elinson, "The Implications of Pentecostal Religion for Intellectualism, Politics, and Race Relations," *American Journal of Sociology* 70 (January, 1965): 414-15.

[21] "Editorial Odds and Ends," *Christian Oracle* 15 (October 27, 1898): 676.

[22] See *Millhands and Preachers* (New Haven: Yale University Press, 1942), pp. 274-84.

For a century poor southern whites and blacks have filled rustic church buildings and revivalists' tents to be reassured of their own personal worth. Poverty, difficult as it might seem, could be transformed into a blessing. "I say it deliberately, and with profound conviction," wrote a nineteenth century preacher, "I am thankful to God that I am a poor man; a thousand times I have felt a profound sense of gratitude to God that my father was a poor man. I think it not unlikely that if in my youth I had had money to spend freely, I should have gone to destruction."[23] Nearly a hundred years later a pentecostal evangelist announced with pride that he ministered largely to "outcasts" because that "puts you on the in-crowd with God."[24] Another evangelist reminded his poor listeners that "Jesus said the world hateth me and the world will hate you also."[25] Powerless, impoverished, and psychically crippled, in their fervent religious meetings the poor in spirit shared moments of ecstasy known only to the children of God. There they found assurance that, indeed, someday, the last would be first.

If dignity was one theme of poor people's religion, even more compelling was its message of help. Sectarian leaders repeatedly reminded the poor that they had no place to turn but to God: "You're not going to be accepted in the church world. Why don't you just go ahead and recognize that you're an outcast? Go ahead and shout the victory and praise God in the spirit. . . . Because God said I'll heal the wounds of the outcast."[26] God could help those who were beyond help. "When you can't meet your financial obligations," shouted evangelist Robert Schambach in a meeting in Miami in 1978, "and when the bank sees you coming they close the door, . . . and all your friends take the phone off the hook, . . . I found somebody that never takes His phone off the hook. In the time of trouble you can call on the Lord and He'll make a way when there is no way."[27] Generations of southern poor whites sang with tired hope, "This World Is Not My Home" and "Oh, Lord, I Need a Friend Like You."

---

[23]"Brevities," *Christian* 18 (October 21, 1880): 1.

[24]Interview with Don Stewart, July 7, 1972. Tape copy in the possession of the author.

[25]Robert Schambach sermon, Miami, Florida, January 28, 1978. Tape copy in the possession of the author.

[26]Don Stewart sermon, Cincinnati, Ohio, July 2, 1972. Tape copy in the possession of the author.

[27]January 28, 1978.

The sectarian gospel was partly pure escapism but it sometimes offered hope in this world, hope for a miracle, hope that could bypass the repressive machinery of society. As if bent by the heavy burdens they carried, hollow-eyed believers in the revival tents of the South swayed back and forth to the hypnotic words, sung over and over again, "Only believe, only believe, all things are possible, only believe." Surely, with God anything was possible. Robert Schambach told his Miami audience: "If you are a child of God you have no business going into the world for help. You'll get help but you gotta pay through the nose. If you can't get money at the bank you can get it from a loan shark. But you're gonna pay back fifteen times as much as you got. And I cannot impress upon you as children of God when you need help you've got the greatest help that this world could ever find and your help is from the Lord."[28] God could bring prosperity, repair broken families, heal sick bodies, and relieve the other crushing burdens of the poor which seemed beyond the power of individual will or social reform.

At its most highly visible levels, as hawked by entrepreneurial revivalists, the sectarian religion of the poor was simplistically escapist, cruelly deceptive, and downright exploitive. The poor were urged to accept their burden rather than overthrow it. And, too often, the earthly hopes of the poor were prodded only at contribution time. Charlatans promised miracles for cash. The miracles smelled of ghetto realism where the last hope was the numbers racket or a floating dice game. Every poor Southerner knew Elmer Gantry well.

From another perspective, the social content of poor people's religion rang true to the oppressed. It was, in fact, their gospel—not preached to them, but preached by them—and it spoke of truths they had learned by experience. Accepting poverty as a permanent fact seemed a perfectly realistic base for a southern Christian message in the early twentieth century. The glorification of suffering supplied a rationale for life for a group of people who otherwise found life uncomfortable and bewildering. The religion of the poor made no altruistic promises that it could not deliver; it simply provided an ideological framework for bleak and barren lives. The facts were clear—life is hard, a poor man's only friend is God, heaven will be a better place to live. That gospel had a market in the South at the turn of the century.

---

[28]Ibid.

Even when charismatic cult leaders exploited the poor, they met very real needs. The illusion of a miraculous blessing from God could become a life-sustaining vision. People who realistically saw a future only of indignity and squalor made use of illusions. A typical high pressure evangelist would argue that he gave the poor man more for his religious dollar than more conventional do-gooders. Show time and fantasies may be more useful than paternalistic lectures and platitudes.

But what of the modern South? Clearly, the gospel of resignation and hope has fewer takers in the Sunbelt. The early twentieth century sects have changed mightily; the meek have seemingly inherited the earth. In Birmingham, Alabama, the Homewood Church of Christ and the Huffman Assembly of God are two of the largest middle-class establishments in the city. The sect-to-denomination evolution has progressed with impressive speed in the South's post-World War II economic boom. The sons and grandsons of southern poor white tenant farmers have built impressive church buildings with familiar names on the outside but with different preaching inside.

Of course, there are vestiges of sectarianism in the South. There are arch-conservative Churches of Christ, tough-minded United Pentecostals, and scores of touring revivalists like David Terrell of Greenville, South Carolina, who regularly canvass the region with the old gospel of worldly pessimism and otherworldly hope. But they look more and more like the religious zealots that one finds in Phoenix and Akron and Seattle. The New South is clearly a less fertile seedbed than the old. Now the richest harvest of new sects is being reaped elsewhere—among urban blacks, in Puerto Rican and Hispanic ghettoes, in California, and, increasingly, in the Philippines and Latin America. The Americanization of the South has fumigated, or polluted, the seedbed. Nearly a hundred years ago a southern sectarian preacher wrote: "With the influx of the northern and foreign element infidel theories, association and influence will come and spread among the working people of our Southern country."[29] And so it came to pass.

---

[29]"A Visit to Chattanooga," *Gospel Advocate* 21 (April 3, 1889): 214.

The Peculiar Peril and Promise of Black Folk Religion

Joseph R. Washington, Jr.

There are two words I wish to place before you as the background against which to set that which is in the foreground of our thinking this afternoon, "The Peculiar Peril and Promise of Black Folk Religion." The first word is from *A Child is Born* by Stephen Vincent Benét. The second word is W. H. Auden's preface to *The Dyer's Hand*. The first word:

> Life is not lost by dying. Life is lost minute by minute, hour by hour, day by dragging day, in all the thousand, small uncaring ways. The smooth appeasing compromises of time, that are King Herod's and King Herod's men, always and always. Life can be lost without vision, but not lost by death. Lost by not caring, willing, going on beyond the ragged edge of time to something no man has seen. You who love money. You who love yourself. And you who have loved and lost and think you can never love again. All the people of this little town. Rise up. Rise up. The loves you have are not enough. Something is loosed to change this shaken world and with it you must change.

The second word:

Whether conditioned by God,
    Or the neural structure—still
All men hold this common creed,
    Account for it as you will
The truth is one,
    And incapable of contradiction
All knowledge that conflicts with itself
    Is poetic fiction.

There are those who claim there is no Black Folk Religion. They do not wish to state thereby there is no religion of Black Folk. Rather, they assert there is nothing distinctive in what is referred to as Black Folk Religion—nothing of intellectual consequence or theological substance unique to it not found in major religions. Hold on to this proposition a moment—label it theologians.

There are those who believe there is no Black Folk Religion, by which they mean to declare that the folk religion of Black People is composed of the same elements as other folk religions—there being precious little in the experience of Black Folk not known in the experience of other folk: all people have known suffering, disillusionment, disappointment, and defeat. Hold on to this proposition a moment—label it mainstreaming.

There are some who affirm there is a Black Folk Religion, and they expressly mean by it a special way of knowing, feeling, seeing, doing, and being that is singular in form and universal in content. Hold on to this proposition—label it Black theologians.

There are still others who contend there is no Black Folk Religion, or religion of Black Folk, because they hold themselves to be of the folk and do not consider themselves religious. Hold on to this proposition, too—label it Black intellectuals.

The truth is one,
    And incapable of contradiction.
All knowledge that conflicts with itself
    Is poetic fiction.

Each of these four propositions asserts as the whole truth that which is part of the truth. There is in truth a Black Folk Religion. It is not dogmatically unique—the theologians are right there. It is not rooted in lore or preliterate stories unrelated to or unfathomable by experiences of other folk: mainstream Christians are right there. It is singular in the form and rhythm of deliverance, but not in content, let alone intent—

Black theologians are half-right there. It is not appreciated or plumbed for its social consequences by many who could make better use of its powerful presence and greater potential: Black intellectuals are revealing here.

There is a Black Folk Religion. This is the case not only because Black Folk are religious and therefore are like all other folk whose nature it is to be religious. There is a Black Folk Religion precisely because Black Folk are concerned about the Ultimate and are ultimately concerned about an ultimate. Black Folk and Black Religion are one, though they are not identical or necessarily interchangeable. It is obvious—there would be no Black Religion were there no peculiar Black Folk. It is not so obvious—there would be no peculiar Black American Folk were there no Black American Folk Religion.

We have alluded to what Black Folk Religion is not. Let us now concisely state what Black Folk Religion is. Black Folk Religion is the quest of Black Folk for freedom, justice, dignity, and equality of opportunity in this world because they know it to be realized in the world to come. Black Folk know themselves to be the people of God, thus they are concerned about *the Ultimate:*

> I've got a home in Dat Rock, Don't you see
> I've got a home in Dat Rock, Don't you see
> Between the Earth and sky, Thought I heard my Savior Cry
> You've got a home in that Rock, Don't you see.

Black Folk are ultimately concerned about realizing freedom, justice, dignity, and equality of opportunity in the here and now:

> If I had my way,
> O Lordy, Lordy,
> If I had my way,
> If I had my way,
> I would tear this building down.

There it is! The peril and promise of Black Folk Religion!

Life is not lost by dying. Life is lost minute by minute, hour by hour, day by dragging day; in all the thousand, small uncaring ways.

Black Folk Religion is the center piece of the Black Community, the heart of Black people—though not their head. There are lesser and greater parts—but no whole apart from Black Folk Religion. Its strength is the weakness of the folk: a people ripped from their roots, labeled black, and denounced unacceptables—forced to be so foolish as to dare and make a society respond to a religion it neither acknowledges as authentic nor accepts as legitimate—a society that gives with one hand, takes with another, and refuses to do the only thing that will do: restructure the society to accomodate Black Folk Religion.

Something is loosed to change this shaken world. And with it
you must change.

It is as if a whole people are forced to stand in the shoes of Joan of Arc. You remember that Peasant symbol of Western Culture? George Bernard Shaw called her *Saint Joan* and in his play placed these words on her lips as she confronted her accusers and despisers, among whom the chief detractor was the head of the Church—the Archbishop:

There is no help, no counsel, in any of you. Yes: I am alone on earth. I have always been alone. My father told my brothers to drown me if I would not stay to mind his sheep while France was bleeding to death: France might perish if only our lambs were safe. I thought France would be friends at the court of the king of France: and I find only wolves fighting for pieces of her poor torn body. I thought God would have friends everywhere, because he is the friend of everyone; and in my innocence I believed that you who now cast me out would be like strong towers to keep harm from me. But I am wiser now; and nobody is any the worse for being wiser. Do not think you can frighten me by telling me that I am alone. France is alone; and God is alone; and what is my loneliness before the loneliness of my country and my God? I see now that the loneliness of God is his strength: what would he be if he listened to your jealous counsels? Well, my loneliness shall be my strength, too: it is better to be alone with God: His friendship will not fail me, nor His counsel, nor His love. In His strength I will dare, and dare, and dare, until I die.

Unwanted and seeking to make a way out of no way—Black Folk are by most accounts a very peculiar people. Take one, for example.Who would be so insensitive as to suggest the holocaust suffered by Indians and Blacks can be weighed in the balance to determine who suffered the most? Still, Indians were offered the opportunity to trade their land and culture for a mess of English pottage, to share in this emerging society on conditions totally unthinkable for them. There was the marriage, too, of John Rolfe and Pocahontas who was accorded royal treatment at the Court of St. James by dent of Captain John Smith. And they who were a once proud people who controlled their land and destiny now have comparatively little more than their pride.

On the other hand, no Black woman was ever even thought to be worthy of an Englishman, let alone allowed to marry a man of social prominence. Blacks were never offered the opportunity to share in more than their productive necessity. But they took this little and along with it the religious underpinnings of this New World. Through their own creative genius, Blacks changed the religious intent, the social fabric, the structure and rules of the society; although the society insists on playing the game by its old rules. Blacks began with twenty and have increased to twenty plus million.

This is a peculiar people, a people of great promise and peril—they have gained less than what they sought, but more than others thought. From whence cometh this will to make "bricks without straw" if not from Black Folk Religion?

The whole of religion is not here. How could it be, for Black Folk Religion was forged out of the language of others by the burning zeal of their own experience. Nevertheless, a whole lot of religion is here—and even a religion of the whole. The folk took the bits and pieces they could snatch from the "Rich Man's table" to create like Lazarus a patchwork of silent but powerful faith. It is a beautiful work to behold, whether or not it is sufficient for all conditions and seasons of men.

Black Folk Religion emerged as a religion seeking wholeness for the community. It was not a religion of salvation for the individual and the community take the hindmost. The voice of the Negro Spirituals which set the theological time, social temper, and political tone was a collective voice and never an individual expression. Out of this halting language and magnificent creation one still finds the real soul of Black Folk.

The community began in religion and centered itself from its inception in God:

In de Lord, In de Lord,
My Soul's been anchored in de Lord
Befo' I'd stay in hell one day,
My soul's been anchored in de Lord

I'd sing an' pray myself away,
My soul's been anchored in de Lord.

The authentic religion of the folk was not divisive. It was not exclusive. It was inclusive of folks without and blacks within who did not share their ground of hope. Black Folk Religion not only stated the universal acceptance of all in general terms,

In His arms He's Got the whole world
He's got the whole world in His arms
He's got you and me Brother
In His arms, He's got you and me Brother,
In His arms, He's got you and me Brother,
He's got the whole world in His arms.

Black Folk Religion also stated the universal acceptance in specific terms, pointing up the common humanity of sinfulness of everyone; God's grace and forgiveness:

The Lord loves a sinner,
The Lord loves a sinner,
The Lord loves a sinner,
And he'll rise in his arms.

Still, each person is responsible to make a decision and thereby be responsive to the all embracing One:

Somebody's knockin' at your door
Somebody's knockin' at your door
Oh, Sinner, why don't you answer
Somebody's knockin' at your door

Knocks like Jesus, Somebody's knockin' at your door
Knocks like Jesus, Somebody's knockin' at your door.

Perhaps the sense of brotherhood wrought out of humiliation, due to racial heritage, reinforced awareness that Christian or no, each and every one must declare

It's me, It's me, O Lord,
Standin' in the need of prayer
It's me, It's me, O Lord
Standin' in the need of prayer
Not my brother, not my sister, not my father, not my mother,
Not my elder, not my deacon, but it's me, O Lord
Standin' in the need of prayer.

Surely the life in this world of the Black man or woman, slave or free, North or South, allowed the community to express its collective pain and burden more in the terms of Golgotha ("My God, My God, Why?") than in the confrontation style of Job:

> Nobody knows de trouble I see
> Nobody knows but Jesus
> Nobody knows the trouble I see
> Glory Hallelujah!

Blacks were acutely conscious of their unacceptableness. They turned in on themselves at times because they could not turn on their oppressors fully, and the price we pay for this self-denigration compares with the cost of our social disintegration today. Still, the Folk religion called Blacks to turn neither upon themselves nor their oppressors but to God:

> I'm gonna tell God how you treat me
> I'm gonna tell God how you treat me
> I'm gonna tell God how you treat me
> Some of these days.

The sense of sin, the understanding that every individual, believer or not, might be wrong in any given circumstance was an ever present word:

> Oh, yes, bow yo' knees upon de groun'
> An' ask yo' Lord to turn you round.

What was the God of Black Folk Religion like? God is love, though love is not God, made visible in Jesus:

> Did you ever see such love before
> King Jesus preaching to the poor,
> I do love the Lord!

Jesus was more than a model—He was Good News:

> O Christians, can't you rise and tell
> That Jesus hath done all things well!

Jesus was not only Lord of Lords and King of Kings, he was the mighty counselor, the source of strength without whom a power failure existed:

> I'm troubled, I'm troubled, I'm troubled in mind
> If Jesus don't help me, I sho'ly will die.

Faith, hope, and charity were constantly expressed, but no attempt was made to hide the sense of loneliness, the burden of never ending trouble in one moment, but, in the next

> I'm so glad, trouble don't last always. . .
> Hallelujah! I'm so glad trouble don't last always.

There were times when escape in and from this world overwhelmed the spirit and dominated all else:

> Steal away, Steal away, Steal away to Jesus
> Steal away, Steal away home—I ain't got long to stay here.

Make no mistake about it, the religion of Black Folk was not deadly or sorrowful even amidst constant pressure, though it was dead serious:

> O bye and bye, bye and bye,
> I'm going to lay down my heavy load.

The note of joy and triumph persisted and dominated. The Old Testament images and figures set the basis for this assurance, that no matter how small their work it could be ultimately effective:

> Little David was a shepherd boy,
> He killed Goliath and shouted for joy.

Even more, the Old Testament hosts made unmistakable the power and presence of God in the most unexpected circumstances:

> Didn't my Lord deliver Daniel,
> Deliver Daniel, Deliver Daniel
> Didn't my Lord deliver Daniel,
> And why not every man!

Thus despite hard times, setbacks, the replacement of one problem with another, the Folk religion was upbeat, confident, determined. In its entirety it declared there was good reason to

> Keep a-inching along
> Keep a-inching along
> Jesus will come by and by!

Good reason, you say?

> Yes, one o' dese mornin's 'bout twelve o'clock
> Dis ol' Worl' am gwineter reel and rock!

How could the folk be so certain?

> My God is mighty man of war, man of war!

So, there was no turning back, no excuses, just

Wade in the water, children
Wade in the water, children
Wade in the water,
God's a-gwinter trouble the water.

In a word, the faith of the folk was rooted in a God of love, mercy, forgiveness, who was at once a God of justice, righteousness, and wrath. This enabled them to trust God and press others in the faith:

We'll stand the storm
It won't be long
We'll anchor by and by!

They had no doubt as to what they were about:

I'm going' to eat at the welcome table,
O yes, I'm goin' to eat at the welcome table
Some of these days, hallelujah!

Thus from the beginning to the end of Black Folk Religion, and all in between there is one clarion call to all:

Walk together, children, Don't get weary
Walk together, children, Don't get weary
Talk together, children, Don't get weary
Sing together, children, Don't get weary
    For de work's most done!

Is that a religion? Is that a heritage? Is that a faith?

Life is not lost by dying. Life is lost minute by minute, hour by hour, day by dragging day, in all the thousand, small uncaring ways.

This is the religion of Black Folk. Its promise abides amidst the peril of many who have whored after other gods: Marxism, socialism, capitalism, nationalism, even Black Power.

Because Black Religion has not delivered on their schedule or in their theoretical framework, many have shunted it to their peril. Black Religion is adaptable, infinitely so, it is not a rigid ideology. It is enormously flexible. It is the living spirit of the people and will respond to creative use in the present. It is a promise in peril, but it will not die until the promise is fulfilled.

To their peril, some have attempted to use Black Religion for their own designs and separate its concern about the Ultimate from its ultimate concern. Minister Malcolm X tried it, to his peril. The Black Muslims tried it, to their peril. The son of a minister, Huey Newton tried it, to his peril. Le Roi Jones who as Immau Baraka the High Priest tried it, to his peril. Paul Robeson tried it, to his peril. W. E. B. DuBois tried it, to his peril.

Men and movements have come and gone, but Black Folk Religion continues. The promise of Black Folk Religion lives on in those who understand it and wed its ultimate concern with its concern about the Ultimate. There is no sacred/secular dichotomy here, they are one as the hand though separate as the fingers. Folk Religion is at its best when the people move from the sanctuaries inspired to wade in the water of this old world.

The promise came to light and life in Minister Martin Luther King, Jr. It is present in Minister Andrew Young. It is present in Minister Walter Fauntroy, the Congressman from Washington, D.C. It is present in Minister Benjamin Hooks, Executive Secretary of the NAACP. It is present in Minister James Joseph, former Under Secretary of the Interior. It is present today, then, in Black religious people who engage in public policy. And it is there in revolution today, too. Ndabaninsi Sithole and Bishop Abel Muzorewa of Zimbabwe bring it to bear in their roles as moderate leaders in the revolution in Rhodesia.

Black Religion is perhaps not unique, but it is different. It is a people determined to walk together, stand the storm, and join together to eat at the welcome table. There is no despair or defeat here, there is peril and promise. The peril and promise was revealed most clearly, possibly, when Black Folk, unlike any other folk, turned their pulpits over to political leaders and just before the Sunday morning sermon allowed a Jimmy Carter and his representatives to speak. Such would be anathema in any mainstream congregation. Some would merely call this action of Black Folk foolish. But the people spoke through the pulpit and Carter was elected. Whatever else, this is "The Peculiar Peril and Promise of Black Folk Religion."

> Life is not lost by dying. Life is lost minute by minute, hour by hour, day by dragging day, in all the thousand, small uncaring ways. The smooth appeasing compromises of time, that are King Herod's and King of Herod's men, always and always. Life can be lost without vision, but not lost by death. Lost by not caring, willing, going on beyond the ragged edge of time to

something more, something no man has seen. You who love money. You who love yourself. And you who have loved and lost and think you can never love again. All the people of this little town. Rise up. Rise up. The loves you have are not enough. Something is loosed to change this shaken world and with it you must change.

Whether conditioned by God, or the neural structure—still
All men hold this common creed, account for it as you will
The truth is one, and incapable of contradiction
All knowledge that conflicts with itself is poetic fiction.

Black Folk Religion . . . Um!

Billy Graham*

William Martin

Revivalists come in for more than their share of hostility and scorn these days. They make easy marks for mimics and satirists, and when an Elmer Gantry or Marjoe Gortner shows up in their ranks, many readily assume they typify the whole batch. Still, young men and, increasingly, young women "get the call" and set out to spread the good news. Most preach in churches and revival centers and a few remaining tents and camp meetings. Some get their own radio or television shows and build a substantial regional or perhaps even national following. But despite a number who would be willing to catch the mantle if it were to fall to them, only once in every two or three generations in America has an evangelist arisen who has not only assumed unchallenged prominence in his field, but has been a dominant force in shaping the religious ethos of his era. In the 1820s and 1830s, Charles Grandison Finney led the revival that Harvard historian Perry Miller credits with playing a major role in welding the new republic together. After the Civil War, Dwight L. Moody served as an anchor to millions of Christians storm-tossed by

---

*Parts of this essay appeared originally in the *Texas Monthly* (March 1978).

Darwinism, German biblical criticism, and a tide of immigrants flooding into the cities with their unfamiliar, non-Protestant ways of thinking and behaving. Despite the comfort Moody offered, the problems not only remained but were exacerbated by a brand new threat that proved to be a mother lode for revivalists: communism. The man who stood in the gap for God in the first two decades of this century was the flashy, acrobatic, baseball-player-turned-preacher, Billy Sunday, the calliope of Zion whose slangy tirades against sin and for prohibition and patriotism moved thousands to "hit the sawdust trail" in his specially constructed wooden tabernacles.

Conservative Christianity fell on difficult years in the Twenties, symbolized by the Scopes trial in 1925, which branded it as a pathetic enclave of anti-intellectual bigotry. Observers of the religious scene pronounced it dead, except for minor rear-guard activity in backwater regions. But, as those who announce the death of religion have always been, the observers were wrong. The Evangelicals not only survived but regrouped, led a dramatic return to religion in the late Forties and Fifties, and, after the Sixties, which set back several other institutions besides Christianity, emerged as what *Time* magazine dubbed a "new Empire of Faith," easily the most vital aspect of contemporary American religion. Given their attitude toward popes and such, Evangelicals are not likely to elect an emperor anytime soon, but if they did, the only possible choice would be Billy Graham, who has been not only the unquestioned symbol but also a dominating influence and power within the Evangelical movement.

There is some irony in my having been asked to place Billy Graham in the context of the southern revivalist tradition. Graham is undeniably a Southerner, and he imbibes heavily of the southern evangelical tradition. But as a revivalist, he probably owes more to northern forebears than to his southern heritage. The South, of course, had a distinctive revivalist tradition. The southern camp meetings at the beginning of the nineteenth century were perhaps the most successful in American history, but the "acrobatic Christianity" and other emotional manifestations that characterized these meetings have been preserved in the pentecostal and charismatic traditions, not in the decorous crusades of Billy Graham. The techniques used by Graham were developed and honed by northerners working in a northern setting. Charles Finney was born in Connecticut, converted in upstate New York, and enjoyed his greatest success as a revivalist in Rochester and Philadelphia. D. L. Moody was a Massachusetts Yankee who accepted Christ in a Boston shoestore, entered full-time Christian work in Chicago, gained national attention for sensational successes in England, and held his greatest meetings in Philadelphia, Chicago, and New York City. Billy Sunday, a native Iowan, played baseball in the National League, found Jesus outside a saloon in Chicago, and saw more people hit the sawdust trail in his New York City campaign than in any other. And Graham himself has headquarters in Minneapolis, came to minor prominence as a Youth for Christ worker in Chicago and California, held his first great revival in Los Angeles, and has reaped a richer harvest of souls outside the South than in his native region. Still, Billy Graham hardly strikes us as an outlander and an examination of his ministry can surely help us understand factors crucial to the success of any major revivalist, northern or southern.

There is, of course, no doubt that Billy Graham has been a success. It is, in fact, quite possible to argue that he is the most successful evangelist in the history of Christianity. Finney, Moody, and Sunday all peaked in less than a decade. But for thirty-five years, Billy Graham has moved along from glory to greater glory, growing in influence and in favor with God and man. He has appeared before more than 50,000,000 people in person and has gathered in over 1,500,000 "inquirers" to sparkle in his heavenly crown. His crowds appear to be as large and the proportion of inquirers as high today as they were in the Fifties. His weekly "Hour of Decision" radio broadcast is heard over 900 stations around the world and he sends telecasts of three or four crusades a year into over 300 metropolitan areas, making them available to a potential ninety percent of the world's television audience. His *Decision* magazine, published in six languages and Braille, has a circulation of almost four million, the largest of any religious monthly and larger than the combined circulation of *The Atlantic, Harper's,* and *Esquire.*

Several of his books, published in dozens of languages, have sold over two million copies apiece. His film company, World Wide Pictures, has produced, in addition to documentary records of crusades and numerous short films, such commercially successful efforts as *Time to Run, The Restless Ones, The Hiding Place,* and *Gospel Road,* an account of the life of Jesus set to the music of Johnny Cash, Joe South, and John Denver. His syndicated column is carried by over two hundred daily newspapers, with a circulation of twenty-nine million. In recognition of these accomplishments, Graham has been *Time's* "Man of the Year," was named in the Gallup Poll's "Ten Most Admired Men in the World," every year between 1951 and 1974 (the poll has not been taken since 1974) and placed second (to Nixon or Kissinger) from 1969-1974. For two years in the mid-Fifties, he received more newspaper and magazine copy than any other person in the U.S., including President Eisenhower. In an informal survey by the liberal ecumenical publication, *Chiristian Century*, conducted to see how many religious leaders were known to American churchgoers, Graham ranked sixty-two percentage points ahead of his nearest colleague. He has received awards for his contributions to race relations and Jewish-Christian relations. He has been a friend of movie stars, athletes, and politicians, including every president since Truman, been honored by the police, military chaplains, the American Football Coaches Association, and the Freedoms Foundation of Valley Forge, Pennsylvania, and is the only living person depicted in stained glass in the national cathedral in Washington, D.C. He has been named "Salesman of the Year" and "Mr. Travel," selected as one of the ten best-dressed men in the nation, received a Horatio Alger Award, recognized as an honorary Indian chief, been Grand Marshal of the Tournament of Roses Parade, appeared on "Laugh-In," and designated "Greatest Person in the World Today" by contestants in the 1976 Miss U.S.A. Beauty Pageant in Niagara Falls. Less tangibly, but more importantly, Billy Graham has come to function as what one writer called "a kind of symbol of consensus among many who think of themselves as the 'Decent People' of America."

Graham and his associates predictably claim that only divine assistance can account for his unparalleled success. It is worth noting, however, that he possesses in abundant measure three additional advantages that, as historian William McLoughlin has shown, appear essential to evangelistic stardom: (1) a simple nondenominational theology; (2) a rational and efficient organization; and (3) a distinctive personality and public style.

Like all authentic Evangelicals, Graham believes the Bible is the true, inspired, and infallible word of God, and as such, the final authority for Christian faith and practice. He acknowledges it contains a great deal of symbolic language and recalls with minor embarrassment a "rather foolish" attempt to delineate the exact dimensions of heaven in one of his youthful sermons. Similarly, his early descriptions of hell and the devil burned more brightly than those of today and he waffles a bit on the nearness of the second coming: "It may be this year, . . . it may be at the end of the century or it may be a thousand years from now." It would be a mistake, however, to conclude that Billy Graham is going soft on doctrine. Those who wish to have fellowship in his crusades and other ventures must accept the deity of Christ, the virgin birth, the atonement, and the resurrection as literal facts. He believes heaven and hell are real places, that the devil is a real person, and even acknowledges that "a few times, but very few," he has personally and successfully commanded "a spirit of divination," (a demon) to come out of a person. And despite his sensible refusal to set dates, he clearly believes The End is a good deal nearer than it ever has been before: "There are about twenty-eight signs that Jesus said to watch for," he told *Newsweek,* "and every one of them is happening."

Though his proclamations have become shorter and more polished, Billy's basic message has not changed through the years. Unlike Norman Vincent Peale and Robert Schuller, who urge us to be as great as we can be through positive and possibility thinking, or Oral Roberts, who promises something good is going to happen to us, or Rev. Ike, who assures us we'll never lose with the stuff he uses, Billy Graham starts on a downer: sinful humanity in rebellion against God. In sermon after article after book he gloomily ticks off the fruits of this rebellion.

> The population increase is frightening . . . our city streets are turned into jungles of terror, mugging, rape, and death. . . . Racial tension is increasing throughout the world. . . . Communism is a dangerous threat . . . God is generally ignored or ridiculed. . . . The age of automation threatens every stage of man's dignity, personality, and individuality. . . . Our western society has become so possessed with sex that it seeps from all the pores of our national life. . . . Divorce has grown to epic proportions. . . . Illegitimate births are at an all time high, venereal disease rages. . . . Eight million persons are suffering from some form of mental illness. . . . Alcoholism is now a national catastrophe. . . . If we can judge our times by the paintings produced by some modern artists, we see indiscriminate splashes of color with no recognizable pattern or design.

Billy is not just making all this up. He reads at least three newspapers a day, has a UPI teletype in his home, and his wife and several assistants clip magazine articles for him and give him books with the good parts already underlined, so he is able to support his views with quotations from the *New York Times* and the *Washington Post* and the *Wall Street Journal,* from *Time* and *Newsweek* and *Reader's Digest,* from the writings of Mark Twain and George Orwell and John Steinbeck and the great Russian novelist Ivan Turgenev, and from Dr. P. A. Sorokin and the famous psychiatrist Sigmund Freud. What's more, he gets a lot of information first-hand, since he has been everywhere and knows just about everybody. People like Dag Hammarskjold and Henry Kissinger and the President and the Pope have told him things are tough all over. And a lot of people whose names he can't even tell us agree, people he met on Oxford Street in London or in the lobby of the Ukraine Hotel in Moscow or somewhere in the jungle, people like senators and a famous film star and a champion athlete and a man on death row and one of Britain's top social leaders and an East European communist official and a man with a Ph.D. from Harvard and one of the world's greatest biochemists and a celebrated Philadelphia neurologist and millionaires in Texas and California who are almost ready to blow their brains out. We are not just dealing with some country preacher. This is a man who can go anywhere and talk to anyone, and they all say the world is going to hell in a handbasket, so we better pay pretty close attention. And now that he mentions it, of course, there does seem to be a certain amount of recognizable imperfection here and there.

The root cause of all these problems is the oldest disease: human sinfulness, passed on to us through the courtesy of Adam and Eve. To compound our fallen state, we are also "sinners by choice" and therefore guilty and doomed to death unless we experience radical change of a sort that cannot come from within ourselves. There is, however, some good news:

> Man—distressed, discouraged, unhappy, hounded by conscience, driven by passion, ruled by selfishness, belligerent, quarrelsome, confused, depressed, miserable, taking alcohol and barbiturates, looking for escapisms—can come to Christ by faith and emerge a new man. This sounds incredible, even impossible, and yet it is precisely what the Bible teaches. . . . His will is changed, his objectives for living are changed, his disposition is changed, his affections are changed, and he now has purpose and meaning in his life. . . . He receives a new nature and a new heart. He becomes a new creation.

What is required, then, is a conversion from old life to new life. Genuine conversion is characterized by repentance (a recognition of and a genuine sorrow for sins) and faith (belief to the point of commitment and surrender). Though conversion is aided by the Holy Spirit, it necessarily involves a voluntary decision by a "free moral agent." A decent amount of emotion—perhaps a flash or two of "strange warmness"— is appropriate but not required, and such charismata as speaking in tongues should not, Graham feels, be regarded as any stronger evidence of conversion than any number of less spectacular manifestations. With or without great tremors of the soul, true conversion brings with it a blessed assurance of salvation, here and hereafter.

Billy not only soft-pedals the doctrines, some of them by no means minor, that divide Evangelicals into denominations, but has been a major force behind a growing evangelical ecumenicity. Before he will accept an invitation to hold a crusade, for example, he insists that a strong majority of the evangelical churches in an area pledge their support. Then, during each crusade, he sponsors a tuition-free school in which as many as 1500 ministers and selected laypeople, representing dozens of denominations, receive fairly intensive instruction in preaching, soul-winning, and church leadership. At a national and international level, he helped start and has remained a major supporter of the highly respected evangelical journal, *Christianity Today*, and has poured millions of dollars into conferences on evangelism throughout the world.

Another aspect of Billy's message that has undoubtedly helped him is that, working a combination Jesus never quite mastered, he manages to comfort the afflicted without afflicting the comfortable. Like Finney and Moody and Sunday, whose list of supporters included such names as Tappan, Dodge, Armour, Wanamaker, Vanderbilt, Morgan, McCormick, and Rockefeller, Graham appeals to wealthy Evangelicals who perhaps need some assurance that the needle's-eye door to the Kingdom of God is not quite so small as they had heard and that wealth, if honestly gotten, is not only permissible but perhaps even a sign God has smiled on them in a special way. They, in turn, take some of the risk out of Billy's ventures. His decision to hold a crusade in New York City in 1969, for example, was reached in the board room of Mutual Life Insurance of New York and the executive committee for the crusade included the board chairman of MONY, his counterpart at Chase Manhattan, and the presidents of RCA and Genesco. Each of these men, incidentally, grew up in far simpler settings and expressed their hope that Graham's efforts in Gotham would help counteract the vice and materialism and spiritual poverty of the city and create an environment more like that in which they had been reared. Billy does not, as some of his critics mistakenly aver, put a divine stamp of approval on all that is American and middle-class; on the contrary, with clenched fist and pointing finger, with glaring eyes and accusing voice, he rings thundering disapproval down on much that he sees. Still, he offers forgiveness and everlasting life to those willing to accept them, without calling on them to make great personal sacrifices. If they love Jesus as he does, they may travel first class, as he does.

The second component of Billy Graham's success is his superb organization. In 1950, after it became clear he was not just another temporary wonder, Graham moved to put his ministry on a solid, businesslike basis. At the suggestion of associate George Wilson, he formed the Billy Graham Evangelistic Association, Inc. (BGEA), a nonprofit corporation headquartered in Minneapolis. Today, with Wilson as chief executive, a staff of approximately 500 processes the mail, donations, and correspondence courses, publishes and distributes *Decision* magazine, and provides counseling-by-mail for those who write Graham with their problems. Also headquartered in Minneapolis are World Wide Publications and the Grason Company, which publish and sell books and records related to Billy's ministry. Films from World Wide Pictures are distributed from Minneapolis, but studios and production facilities are located in Burbank, California. The Walter Bennett Agency in Philadelphia handles radio and television for the ministry, as it has since the Hour of Decision went on the air in 1950. In addition to these, the Graham organization maintains smaller operations in London, Paris, Sydney, Hong Kong, Winnipeg, and Kyoto.

Nowhere is the rationality, thoroughness, and efficiency of Graham's organization more apparent than in the planning and execution of its crusades. Not surprisingly, he receives many more invitations to hold crusades than he can possibly accept. In the past, the strategic importance of the city in question was a key criterion. Is it a major population center? Does it have great political or economic importance? Will a crusade there win coverage in the newspapers of other cities? Today, because Graham's crusades are televised for national presentation, cities are selected for their suitability as a studio. Politicians have learned to do the same things for the same reasons. As the Reverend Charles Riggs, one of Graham's longtime crusade directors, explained, "Since your big audience is on television, it is smarter to go somewhere where you will get better support and where it won't cost you as much. A crusade in the South, for example, is many times less expensive than one in the North. In the North, things cost a lot more, labor unions run the cost up, whereas down in the South you get things donated." For these reasons, Graham has turned in recent years to cities such as Jackson, Alburquerque, and Lubbock.

Once an invitation has been accepted, representatives from the host city form a nonprofit corporation that will be responsible for financing the crusade and developing the necessary organization. Several months before a crusade begins, the Graham association sends members of its team to open an office in the host city and involve as many people as possible in various facets of the crusade. Committees, choruses, Bible classes, orientation sessions for ushers and counselors, prayer groups, and other activities arranged by the team involve thirty to forty thousand, and sometimes as many as eighty thousand people in various facets of a crusade. With that accomplished before he hits town, Billy Graham really doesn't have to worry much about drawing a crowd.

To those who attend a crusade or view it on television, the pay-off of all this effort seems to come when hundreds, sometimes thousands of people stream from the stands to make their "decisions for Christ." Most perhaps imagine that Graham and his team have now done their job, have accomplished what they sought. As one looks more carefully into and behind this scene, however, it becomes apparent that the same kind of efficiency and skill that produced this crowd of inquirers will now process them through intricate and well-oiled machinery designed to lead them from decision to discipleship.

As Graham offers the invitation, the aisles fill not only with inquirers, but also with counselors. Insofar as possible, a counselor seeks out an inquirer of the same sex and approximately the same age group and asks him or her to check the item on a decision card that most nearly matches the reason he or she has come forward—first-time commitment, rededication, special problem, etc. After a two- or three-minute review of the gospel, the counselor presents the inquirer with a small packet of materials, which includes the Gospel according to John, a Bible-study lesson, a devotional guide, and several Scripture verses printed on small cards to facilitate memorization. Finally, the counselor helps the inquirer complete the decision card, suggests they pray together, and urges the new friend in Christ to get in touch if any problems arise during the next few days.

Within minutes, the decision cards are transferred to what is known as the "Co-Labor Corps," a group of 200-300 workers housed in an armory or gymnasium and looking like a cross between a political convention, the newsroom of a large metropolitan daily newspaper, and a Christian beehive. There the cards are sorted into broad categories, such as denomination and type of decision, then passed on to researchers who fill in missing items with the help of zip-code books, criss-cross directories, and special computer printouts prepared by the crusade team. "If a person comes here from Louisiana," a supervisor told me, "and puts down his street address, chances are we can figure out what church and what pastor we should notify concerning his decision."

After retyping, the card, together with an explanatory letter, is then sent to a pastor who has been named by the inquirer, whose members invited the inquirer, whose participating church is nearest the inquirer's residence, or who has been specially selected by a "decision committee" charged with making such assignments. Though Graham often speaks well of Roman Catholics and they of him, he still regards his ministry as distinctly Protestant and does not assign cards to Roman Catholic churches. Neither would he honor a request to contact a pastor of such cults as the Church of Scientology or the Reverend Sun Myung Moon's Unification Church.

These letters are then metered, sorted according to zip code, taken to a special branch of the post office, and delivered in the next morning's mail. This means that for virtually every person who responds to Graham's invitation in an evening service, some pastor in a sixty-mile radius will have received a letter by noon the following day, urging him to contact the inquirer, take appropriate action, and report back to a follow-up committee.

The Graham organization is sensitive to the criticism that revival fires rapidly burn out and seeks to sustain them as long as it can. Beginning the day after the crusade closes, the radio station that has carried the prayer broadcasts begins a series of morning and evening programs dealing with what it means to be saved and how to live as a Christian. Three weeks later, all inquirers are contacted by telephone and asked about any difficulties they may have had, urged to attend church and join a Bible study group, and encouraged in the continuing struggle against sin.

The fact that a high proportion of inquirers list a pastor or church on their decision cards raises an issue that has been around since D. L. Moody began to keep track of responses to his preaching. Newspaper reporters at the revivals of the great mass evangelists, including Graham, have repeatedly noted that the "sinners" who responded to those evangelists' persuasive entreaties have often carried well-worn Bibles and looked suspiciously like people who were not being exposed to organized religion for the first time. Only about half of Billy Graham's inquirers— in Bible Belt areas, the proportion may be as low as a third—claim they are making a first-time commitment to Christ. And, of course, a high proportion of the first-timers are children who would eventually have made the same decision had Graham never come to town. Some of the believers who "rededicate" their lives in a crusade are doubtless genuine reprobates, dragooned into the stadium against their will or perhaps come to scoff and moved instead by terror or love to repent and turn from their evil ways. More, I am fairly certain, are people of tender conscience who feel they have not done all they might to win souls, or have been more concerned with their own affairs than with their Father's business, or who feel guilty because they daydream during the pastor's sermon. Still, this does not mean Graham's results are spurious or insignificant. Like the decision to attend college or to marry, a decision to say "I am now ready to assume the responsibility of living as a Chrisitan" is not less momentous simply because it is an expected part of one's life agenda. Similarly, if a substantial number of church folk whose light has begun to dim are plugged back into their systems on a high-voltage line, the crusade has performed an important function, from the perspective both of the individual and the systems in question. To dismiss revival decisions because the people who make them are not considered by the observer to be sufficiently sinful is to miss a significant point.

Any preacher with the sense to keep his theology simple and the foresight to surround himself with able associates could probably achieve moderate success. But these alone do not produce an evangelistic superstar, any more than a good piano and high-quality lessons will turn out a Horowitz. If it were otherwise, we could recall more easily the names of some of the dozens of young evangelists who have been heralded as "the next Billy Graham." What does Graham have that makes him so appealing to so may? He is attractive and forceful and confident, to be sure, but one could hardly describe him as colorful; in fact, he seems almost dynamically bland. He seldom turns a memorable phrase, his mind seems innocent of complexity, and his observations are thoroughly predictable. All of us know several people who are intrinsically more interesting. And yet he is undeniably an authentic All-American Hero.

In accounting for Graham's success, observers have often noted two crucial public-relations bonanzas that occurred early in his career. During the fourth week of his 1949 Greater Los Angeles Revival, William Randolph Hearst, who had admired the young evangelist's work with Youth for Christ, sent the editors in his influential chain of newspapers a two-word telegram: "Puff Graham." And they did. A flood of publicity followed, including features in major news magazines and two wire services. A few weeks later, Henry Luce came to Columbia, South Carolina, to hear Graham in a crusade and pledge the support of *Time, Life,* and *Fortune.* After that, Billy could go wherever he wanted and set his own terms. But despite the enormous boost they provided, it is important to remember that Hearst and Luce were not making a random selection or engaging in creation *ex nihilo.* Their empires had been built on a singular genius for matching a communications medium to the receptivity of a mass audience, and when they found Billy Graham, they saw a man who not only had that same talent, but was himself the medium.

People are drawn to Graham for his personal style and character. He is kind, personable, charming, and, I believe, absolutely sincere. He is apparently even humble, expressing wonder at what he has done, awe at the responsibility of his position, and doubt that he is up to it. He works hard—so hard, in fact, that he has suffered physically. He has high blood pressure, can perform no heavy lifting, has thrombophlebitis, and a recurring intestinal ailment, and from time to time has had to slow down because of an eye problem related to exhaustion.

Graham leads a life of considerable personal discipline, rising early, reading five Psalms and one chapter of Proverbs, watching the Today show during breakfast, spending an hour in Bible study after breakfast, then working, jogging, writing, and closing the day with another round of devotions—the very sort of existence most evangelical Christians feel they should lead but so seldom manage. Because they believe he is one of them, yet the best of them, Billy's words carry a special authority. He is so consistent, so sure, so reassuring, in a time when so much of life is none of these.

He also appeals to the people in the pews because they feel at home with him intellectually. His humor is obvious, as if gleaned from "Laughter is the Best Medicine" and "Today's Chuckle." He loves sentimental stories like the one about the mediocre football player who starred on the day his blind father died because "it was the first time my dad ever got to see me play." And though he occasionally laments the fact that he never took time to earn a doctorate, he does not pretend to be a theologian or Biblical scholar. In fact, he has openly admitted that when he suffered a period of doubt in 1949, he resolved it not by working through the problems that troubled him but by making a conscious decision not to think about them any more. "If that be intellectual suicide," he says, "so be it." This simplicity pervades the literature Graham publishes and apparently reflects the concerns of his readers. A question-and-answer column in *Decision* magazine regularly deals with such chestnuts as why people no longer live as long as Methuselah did, where the sons of Adam and Eve got their wives, and whether the Garden of Eden can be located on a map. Thus, what Benard Weisberger has said of Charles Finney may be equally true of Billy Graham: "He did not study the popular mind; he had it."

It would be fatuous, of course, to imply that Billy Graham is the Hero of All the People. Archfundamentalist Carl McIntire, outraged by what he regards as a damnable penchant for compromise, calls Graham "the greatest disappointment in the Christian world." To liberal Christians he epitomizes a religious and, by implication, political outlook singularly inappropriate to the structures and needs of contemporary societies. And to others, cynical toward any who profess to live by lofty ideals and bone-weary at repeated disappointment in those they had dared trust, Billy Graham is simply not believable. In time, they are confident, he will be exposed and they will dance at his disgrace.

Graham's religious critics have scored him for an overemphasis on the personal sins that have traditionally drawn the fire of revivalists and most evangelical and fundamentalist preachers: alcohol, drugs, sex (including rape, adultery, homosexuality, abortion, and pornography), and crime. It is an easy matter to dismiss these as "frontier morality" and to pretend Graham and his colleagues are tilting at windmills. But, as a matter of fact, these are *real* problems and they are *social* problems. Still, one could wish Dr. Graham were equally as concerned with such matters as unjust distribution of resources, social structures that give rise to criminal behavior in both the lower and upper classes, and the systematic arrangements that help perpetuate the disadvantaged position of various social groups. Basically, Graham's view has been the classical revivalist and evangelical view: institutions will not change until the hearts of the individuals who constitute them have changed. There is, of course, an element of truth in this, but there is also an element of untruth. Minds often change as a consequence of prior changes in institutions. Fifteen to twenty years ago, many white folk in this region felt, deep in their heart of hearts, that reading, riding, and eating in the same vicinity with colored people were experiences they could do without. Today, racial integration in public places, brought about largely by Supreme Court decisions and congressional acts, has become institutionalized and accepted—one need not claim perfection to acknowledge real change. Institutions and hearts have both changed, but the institutions changed first, and when religious and political conservatives insist that change happens only in the other direction, they are mistaken.

It would be unfair, however, to contend that Billy Graham shuts his eyes completely to institutional and structural problems, or even that he always takes a conservative line on such matters. In the early years of his ministry, he side-stepped the racial issue but by 1953 insisted his crusades be completely open to all races, even in the Deep South, and refused invitations to South Africa for years. When he finally held crusades in Durban and Johannesburg in 1973, blacks constituted at least half the audience and sat where they wanted to. At the risk of offending a sizable segment of his supporters, Graham toured Latin America with Dr. Martin Luther King, Jr., and his organization prepared a series of spot announcements for use in the South, urging parents to "obey the law" on school integration.

In 1971, Billy held crusades in Cleveland, Chicago, and Oakland, all chosen because they had been the site of severe racial disturbance and he hoped the crusade might have a healing effect. Many of his critics, of course, would argue that what he offers is not true healing, but an anesthetic of the sort Marx had in mind when he spoke of religion as "the opium of the people" and that perhaps what was needed was not a painkiller but therapy far more radical. Graham and his followers, however, seem to feel that the only good radical is a saved one, like the black football player who stated at a Tennessee crusade that, "I'd be the most militant man in the country today if I hadn't found Jesus."

Though he repeatedly insists his primary concern is for the salvation of individual souls, Graham has given indication of growing concern for social structures. In his welcoming address at the 1974 Lausanne Conference on World Evangelism, he told the delegates he believed in "political freedom, the changing of unjust political and social structures where needed, and where possible equal justice for all." In recent years, *Decision* magazine has taken a somewhat more positive attitude toward Christian efforts to influence social legislation and editor Sherwood E. Wirt describes the traditional contention that politics cannot solve the problems of the world as "precisely the kind of cop-out that gave Evangelicals a bad name in society, and turned our 'odor of sanctity' into a stench in the nostrils of God."

The most scathing criticism leveled at Graham in recent years, of course, has been directed at his perceived role as "High Priest of American Civil Religion" and, more specifically, as "court chaplain" to the Nixon administration. Though perhaps not entirely fair to him, Graham's political predilections—against militancy of most sorts, against disruptive protests, against involvement of the church in radical social action, in favor of rugged individualism and the work ethic—made it quite easy and natural for him to say, with complete sincerity, precisely what Nixon wanted said and what his conservative Republican constituents wanted to hear. I do not believe Billy Graham would pander to just any president who happened to be in power. In lending his considerable support to the Nixon presidency, he was expressing the same views he had held publicly since the beginning of his ministry.

Graham's friendship with Nixon goes back to the late Forties, when Strom Thurmond introduced him to the young congressman from California. Whatever one may conclude about the depth of Nixon's piety, his background had prepared him for Billy's brand of religion. Though his Quaker heritage is often noted, what is less well-known is that the particular sect in which Nixon was reared was not greatly unlike the fundamentalist and evangelical churches from which Graham draws most of his following. The friendship deepened over the years. Nixon has credited Graham with having encouraged him to run for the Presidency in 1968, and when he secured the nomination, Billy sat in on the session at which Spiro Agnew was selected as Nixon's running mate—I like to believe they did not pray about the matter and am comforted to know that Graham's first choice was Mark Hatfield. Though he did not publicly endorse Nixon, the evangelist did appear as a member of the television audience on question-and-answer shows and when the wire services reported that his absentee ballot had carried Nixon's name, the candidate's camp readily exploited the information.

Graham once insisted Nixon would "never, never try to use me politically," a claim that seems touchingly naive in retrospect, probably even to Graham. By inviting him to pray at the inauguration and preach at the White House, by sitting on the platform at the 1970 Knoxville Crusade, and by generally letting it be known he was on the same side as Billy and the angels, Nixon drew heavily on Graham's enormous appeal and influence with conservative voters. As the corruption in the administration came to light, Graham acknowledged Nixon may have exploited their relationship, but refused to abandon his disgraced friend, a stance that required considerable character and was hardly motivated by a desire to enhance his own public image. "When a friend is down," he said, "you don't go and kick him—you try to help him up."

Since Watergate, Graham has conceded that if the president told lies, it was a sin, and has called for national repentance "from the White House to your house." His critics, including Evangelicals, have observed pointedly that when David took Bathsheba and sent her hapless husband off to die in battle, the prophet Nathan did not simply preach a series of lessons decrying immodesty, adultery, and abuse of power, but strode into David's presence and said accusingly, "Thou art the man!" But Nathan was a prophet and not an evangelist. Prophets are sent away from the court, cast into jails and cisterns, and threatened with death. Evangelists, like salesmen, must never make a potential customer feel uncomfortable in a way that might risk loss of the sale.

Graham's religious and political beliefs have always given his ideological opponents plenty to shoot at, but the cynics among his detractors have been less fortunate. He has avoided any hint of the sexual scandal that has tainted several other ministries by making certain he is never alone with a woman other than his wife or close relative, even for a few minutes. And, throughout most of his ministry, he has been a model of financial integrity. At the close of his 1950 Atlanta Crusade, the *Atlanta Constitution* carried two photographs side by side. One showed Graham waving goodbye to the city. The other showed money bags containing $9,000 collected as a "love offering" for the five weeks the evangelist had spent in the city. The insinuation rankled Graham and his team and he quickly accepted a recommendation that he scrap the love-offering system and place himself on an annual salary to be set by his board. At that time, his salary was set at $15,000; at present, it is $39,500.

In addition to his salary, of course, he receives full expenses while away from home, plus income from his writings. He has also inherited land valued at $420,000 and sold other inherited properties for $250,000. Although he has established trust funds for his children, much of the considerable income from his books has gone either to charitable causes or back into his ministry. He estimates, for example, that he gave away approximately $600,000 in 1977. He is thus financially comfortable, but has repeatedly refused to take advantage of his position to build a personal fortune. His organization owns no airplane or stable or expensive automobiles; Graham's two personal cars are a Volvo and a Jeep.

Because the BGEA is incorporated as a church, it is not required to file an IRS return and did not, until 1978, publish a financial statement for the benefit of its donors. Still, Billy's salary and rough estimates of the ministry's income and overall expense have not been dark secrets, and until mid-1977 virtually every investigation into Graham's finances found him and his organization without spot or blemish. In 1977, however, the *Charlotte Observer*, Billy's hometown paper, revealed the existence of a $22.9 million fund that, though undeniably part of the Graham organization, had been "carefully shielded from public view." The implications embarrassed Graham but he managed to show that the fund was legal, had apparently never been used for his or anyone else's personal gain, and, despite an admittedly low profile, was not a "secret" fund. Having apparently absorbed the lesson that, despite Jesus' instructions to his disciples to be "wise as serpents and harmless as doves," folk are still apt to be wary of serpents, Graham pledged to publish an annual financial statement to avoid such complications in the future.

The strains of dueling with the devil for decades have wearied Billy just a bit. He admits he is sometimes tired and lonely and, exhibiting clear confidence in the message he brings, claims that the prospect of death sometimes seems welcome: "I would be very happy," he told one interviewer, "if the Lord would say it's time to go home. I'm looking forward to it because the pressures of my particular life are very heavy and I get very homesick for heaven. . . . But I don't want to be a cop-out either. I want to stay and do what He wants me to do."

Obviously, he does not think the Lord is ready for him to hang up his Bible just yet. He admits he has made some inquiries about a crusade in the Soviet Union and says he might even accept an invitation to preach in

Rome if the colosseum could be fixed up and made safer for Christians than it was the last time they used it extensively. If his health holds and the Lord tarries, we can reasonably expect Billy Graham to remain active for at least another ten years. There are plenty of willing candidates around, but I see no one likely to step into his pulpit when he retires. My personal prediction is that the current evangelical revival will soon level off, then enter a gradual decline for several decades, at least in this country. Eventually, some young man or woman with the right combination, a combination easy to describe but apparently hard to embody, will arise to join the elite ranks of the world-class heavyweight evangelists. It may be that developments in communication and transportation will enable the New Light to shine more brightly than Billy ever could, just as radio and television and jet power have enabled him to reach more people than his predecessors have dreamed possible. But unless and until that happens, and it is by no means a sure thing, Billy Graham, whatever we may think of evangelists and the gospel they preach, has to be regarded as the best who ever lived at what he does, "a workman," as the Scripture says, "that needeth not to be ashamed."

The Shape and Shapes of Popular Southern Piety

Samuel S. Hill, Jr.

It is well-known that Christian piety abounds in the American South and is of the kind generally called Evangelical Protestantism. Less well-known is the fact of a considerable diversity within that species of Evangelicalism. A major reason for the lack of awareness of that diversity is the lack of first-hand exposure to southern modes of religious expression. Accordingly, this paper essays to describe the varieties of southern religious experience and to claim for the phenomenon an admirable richness. It would seem appropriate to register those goals in part through the use of three familiar and favorite regional forms, autobiography, biography and narrative, and spiritual appeal. The sensitive reader will perceive that those translate as testimony, story-telling, and preaching, respectively, in the typical practice of the southern religious. Medium and message are both important, since choices in one area (either one) condition the choices in the other.

A standard definition of Evangelicalism, as it took classic shape in antebellum southern life—and is supposed by many to be today, whether in the South, the American North, or elsewhere in the world—is offered by Donald G. Mathews:

> ... the Christian life is essentially a personal relationship with
> God in Christ, established through the direct action of the
> Holy Spirit, an action which elicits in the believer a profoundly
> emotional conversion experience. This existential crisis, the
> *New Birth* as Evangelicals called it, ushers the convert into a
> life of holiness characterized by religious devotion, moral
> discipline, and missionary zeal.[1]

In his extended analysis Mathews goes beyond most students of southern
Evangelicalism (and other branches of that Protestant family) in seeing
that it is also "social process" and that it possesses a strong ethical sense,
personal and social. Nevertheless, as he himself notes, the evangelical
passion was for the creation of disciplined individuals rather than a good
society. And this has been more emphatically the case since the Civil War.

The key terms of the most traditional southern forms of
Evangelicalism are indeed "personal relationship with God," "through
direct (divine) action," culminating in a "profoundly emotional
conversion experience" called the "new birth," resulting in a "life of
holiness" in which the identifying marks are "devotion," "discipline,"
and "zeal." So, what Mathews says of antebellum Evangelicalism is
accurate. Error creeps in at the point where an analyst may suppose or
aver that it is still only that same way. Since World War II in particular, the
long-standing fact of diversity within southern Evangelicalism has been
apparent. It may be, of course, that for fear of doing violence to
Evangelicalism, a form of Christianity likely to be found wherever in the
world that religion is found, we should simply speak of southern piety,
without insisting on classifying all its major forms under Evangelicalism.
But that generic title is in standard usage and does rather accurately
describe popular regional religion.

We may take a leaf from Mathews' own notebook and be certain that
so dynamic, driven, ambitious, responsive, adaptive, and circumspect a
tradition as southern Evangelicalism would spawn its own offspring over
time. It has done so, as it has passed from Reconstruction to the era of
industrialization, next to the Great Depression, then through a major
war followed by economic progress, demographic shifts and growth, and
the major social dislocation attendant upon the 1954 Supreme Court

---

[1]Donald G. Mathews, *Religion in the Old South* (Chicago: University of Chicago
Press, 1977), p. xvi.

decision concerning desegregation. The antebellum style of Evangelicalism is very much with us today, and still predominant, although more as "modern revivalism" than as simpler frontier forms. But there is a variety of southern religious experience, even within Evangelicalism.

Let me begin to demonstrate this by turning, as Southerners are wont to do, to my own religious experience. The questions that were raised in my meditations on Christian meaning are likely to be transparent to the regional religious mind. I should note at the outset that perhaps all that distinguishes mine from a typical recitation is a capacious inclination to reflect, which results from the extensive training in theology and religion required of a professional student in the field; and secondly, from a regionally atypical concern to view such experience not as a one-time occurrence but as a longitudinal development. Notwithstanding the slightly special circumstances of my own experience, I believe this autobiographical discussion may reveal something of the orientation and dynamic of popular southern piety. It has a chance of showing some "southern soul" through pointing to several assumptions and basic teachings common to the region's religious life which are not subject to neat classification in the index of a theology textbook.

Born into a Baptist minister's family which had roots and residence in Virginia and Kentucky, I was nurtured in the Sunday School and converted and baptized at age eight. I was never unhappy about going to church as frequently as Sunday mornings and evenings and Wednesday evenings every week. It is true that I was never offered the choice of participating or not, and never shown any alternative. But I did more than take the family's religious patterns for granted; I entered in rather joyfully and with meaning. To this day in my fifty-fourth year, I have never not been a churchman nor considered rejecting the tradition or even becoming inactive within it.

In March, 1973, I was confirmed into membership in the Episcopal Church. To some of my relatives and friends that must have seemed a radical break with my past as a lifelong Southern Baptist who was ordained to the ministry at age nineteen; to others it may even have smacked of defiance and rejection. Nothing of the sort was taking place. There was no semblance of repudiation. I knew very well what was happening that day, because the Baptists had nurtured me in the need for "rededication of life." They teach that one may very well need to do such a thing periodically and do it in concrete, public acts. I had found in the

Episcopal presentation of Christianity the means to deepened understanding and commitment and was responding to that. Occasionally now a member of a church class I teach or some other good friend will accuse me of being a "Southern Baptist Episcopalian." This is accurate, for I carry over into my new (lay) style of churchmanship the same sensibilities of guilt, presence, joy, and intensity imbued in me by the Baptists.

But there has been a great deal of movement—which, one hopes, adds up to growth. What has occasioned that passage from Baptist to Episcopal, from evangelical to liturgical, from immediacy to mediation, from biblicism to sacramentalism, and so on? (The language of these pairings is more suggestive than precise.) Some particular issues, concerns, and questions may indeed be isolated as factors in the movement, and they, as a type, may be seen as a natural outgrowth of the reflective life of an academician. What is significant, however, is how relatively small the change has been: from the piety of an unmediated individualistic experience to the piety of liturgical worship in a corporate setting. That bears reiteration: from one sort of piety to another. Both interpret Christianity as primarily encounter with the holy.

Grappling with at least six issues helped prompt the movement which had been building toward its crescendo over many years. (1) During my late college and early seminary years, I was active in preaching "youth revivals." While that activity never possessed me with a clear sense of permanent vocation, I carried it on with some joy and basic integrity. Late in that period, however, I realized—alas, one night in the midst of preaching a sermon—that I was asking people *to do* something which *had been done* for me. That is to say, I was making the evangelistic appeal, *you accept* Christ, *you receive* His salvation, *you step out* and come forward, *you let go and let God* have his way in your heart, when I *had done* nothing of the sort. Yet I felt myself no less seriously Christian for not having "done" anything. William James would doubtless classify me a once-born type (though he and I both are quick to acknowledge the existence of the twice-born). But my objectivist position—which had come from God knows where—could not allow indefinitely for the continuation of such an undertaking. My leadership as a Christian, whether clerical or lay, had to grow out of and be at one with the nature of my own piety.

(2) Why does the Bible have authority? No issue could be more central for a Baptist boy from the South. Yet I had never ruminated the

question, not even in college or seminary, with much cogency. Respecting Scripture's authority, I assumed something like: it has authority because it is the authority. Then in a graduate seminar on a quite different subject, someone casually remarked that he believed the Bible because he saw himself on every page of it. Well, that throw-away remark unleashed a flood of questionings and searchings (which still haven't stopped). Almost instantaneously, the where-do-you-draw-the-line issue with reference to what is "true" ceased being an issue at all. (It had been suspect to me for several years, but its rejection was awaiting formulation.) I began to refine old issues and questions concerning the nature and authority of the Bible, a process which eventuated in my seeing that the Bible must be interpreted in dramatic categories, as distinct from historically or dogmatically infallible ones. In other words, the Bible is set within our history and its message must be seen as having to do with the living of life. The result? I take it far more seriously than when I also took it literally; at any rate I hope and believe so.

(3) Anyone nurtured in a communion which emphasizes direct and intensely personal religious experience is bound to be caught short by another question which also I heard in a graduate seminar: do you have to *know* that you are experiencing the reality of God to be actually experiencing it? Immediately I knew the answer was "no" although no one in my tradition had ever had reason to raise it. I learned that day that a person's theology often extends beyond his formulation of it. But with respect to the question itself I was prompted to consider as never before the nature of religious experience, and concluded that intense feelings need not accompany genuine encounter. How can one know that he is in relationship with God? Does a feeling or an awareness suffice—or even is it necessary—in order to demonstrate the reality of God or at least of one's relationship with Him? I came to the position that both the reality and the human perception of it are greater than and not identical with "religious experience." This had the effect of deemphasizing conscious awareness, especially as test, proof, and validation, and of expanding the range of divine activity in one's life.

(4) The question of assurance—how can one know that he is forgiven, is accepted by the all-righteous Lord? In the tradition of my youth, that was a—no, *the*—salient question. The logic moved from: one is a sinner in urgent need of forgiveness; *to* one accepts this gracious gift provided through the benefits of Christ's death; *to* one knows for sure that he has been pardoned hence has been redeemed by

God for life in Him now and with Him forever. What took place in my reorientation was a shift away from the view that assurance is a problem that has to have a solution, or the response to a need requiring a definite treatment and cure. The new understanding placed me in a posture of trust, of responsible indifference, of not concerning myself with the issue but rather throwing myself on God's mercy, regarding His concern for me as the context of life.

(5) How to read the Bible? One reared a Southern Baptist just took for granted the authoritative character of the Bible. Whether intended or not, my teachers communicated that it was mostly "divine," "out of this world," given to people here from the One who is beyond. Then in a Baptist seminary I learned that, to take one basic case, the doctrine of the Trinity was hammered out over a long period of time, rather than being formulated in Scripture itself. The raw materials of the Bible were fashioned into an "official" doctrine after much debate and study in 325 A.D. (and secondarily, 451). I inferred from this that the Bible is "in history," a part of the same process which also is the context of my own times. This made me some kind of "catholic Christian" while calling for dramatically revised ways of seeing the Bible's authority and reading its contents. The Church is in history; so is the Bible. Furthermore, that history is qualitatively the same as my own.

(6) What is different about the South and its popular religious forms? The aggregation of the preceding five questions, plus several others of like order, produced a clear sense of regional cultural identity as I gradually came into contact with wider Christendom and the vast Christian tradition. In wrestling with this, I came to see the cultural context of my own religious faith, and presumably of everyone else's. In fact, I soon came to regard historical-cultural setting and conditioning as inevitable. However, this inference did not generate any notion of religion as essentially a "dependent variable," as something absolutely determined by this-worldly forces. In rejecting the latter position, which is embraced by many of my fellow students of religious organizations, I have no doubt reflected the positive power of the very religious tradition about which I have raised so many questions and with which I am no longer formally identified.

This list of questions and issues, it may be apparent and should be noted, grow rather naturally and easily out of a southern EP experience. They are posed by that tradition, either as extension of its logic or as displacement of its concerns and answers in favor of others. But I should point out, more briefly than I would like, that these insights surfaced as real people as often as they did as mere questions or issues arising from reflection. As a child and young adult I knew southern EPs who held wide-ranging positions. Among them were people who were: pacifists; knowledgeable about Christian history; unconcerned with rewards and punishments; dedicated to eradicating racial segregation and discrimination; much in touch with the currents of thought in the wider Christian and secular worlds; censorious of guilt-based religion; Chrisitian humanists of one sort or another; disposed to poetic, dramatic interpretations of Scripture; fundamentally ecumenical; critical of much in the southern EP tradition; particularists without being exclusivists; incipiently sacramental; at one and the same time emotional pietists and tough-minded intellectuals; both light-hearted and urgent in their grasp of Christian faith; affirmative toward Jews and their religious identity; appreciative of the Roman Catholic tradition; not "in this thing" either for what they could get out of it or because they felt obligated to be; dedicated Christians but without a conversion experience; affiliated with the southern EP tradition more because they were at home in it than because they knew and were anxious to defend its ideology.

Incarnations like these highlight the inadequacy of definitions of Evangelical Protestantism and of lists of trouble points prepared by theologians or social scientists. There is a vast and rich diversity. Withal, some general descriptions and characterizations can be made. This is due to there being: (a) a way of thinking about Christianity called Evangelical Protestantism; and (b) a distinction between the popular EP of the South and other forms of that family of Christianity prevalent in the northern sections of this country. Such a thing as southern EP does exist; only it is somewhat different from what many suppose and quite varied.

The best generic description of EP refers to its foundation as a "theology of unmediated encounter." This communicates the fundamental point that a genuine, conscious, and powerful relationship exists between the God of heaven and the individual believer. He or she is continually aware of the presence of the Lord and decisively committed to following obediently. The conviction of the Lord's reality, direction, and presence is self-confirming. It is thus "unmediated," occurring person-to-person, without significant reliance on worship forms, clergy certification, sacramental participation, doctrinal propriety, or ecclesiastical legitimation.

Two ways of clarifying "unmediated" come to my mind and may be helpful to others. The first is through an analogy from the commercial airline industry, specifically, the distinction between "non-stop flights" and "direct flights." For most Christians historically the way in which God and people meet is like the "direct" flight, in which the passenger goes straight from point A to point C without changing aircraft, but lands at point B en route. The analogy consists in the fact that forms are used and prized, indeed deemed essential, partly because they are inevitable. The reality of God is communicated and made effective through symbols, writings, liturgies, offices, personality, and formularies, none of which is viewed as obtrusive or superfluous and all of which are seen as vehicles of the movement of God toward people. By contrast, in EP the "non-stop" analogue is appropriate. The Lord Himself acts directly in history and in our history, speaks directly to us, is closer to us than the air we breathe and the water we drink. Forms may exist and be used, but they are in theory expendable and are viewed suspiciously for fear they may become crutches or barriers. The EP knows nothing so intimately and purely as the Lord and His will.

The second illustration is that for the Evangelical God's reality and presence come to us in *pointed*—specific, identifiable—fashion, rather than in *diffused* fashion. In considering this, it helps to imagine the difference between a vector come to its point and a series of continuous parallel lines each with an arrow on its tip. In the case of the vector or the ("pointed") case, which means EP, you know whatever you know, the truth or the Lord Himself, or what you are being led to do, with precision, exactly, for sure. Accordingly, Evangelicals "know more" than other kinds of Protestants; far less is left in the realm of mystery. This is due to the acceptance of a theory of knowledge, or epistemic position, which assesses truth as precise and exact; it thus is possible for a perception to be precise concerning something which is precise.

Consistent with those descriptions, we may proceed now to characterize EP. (1) It lives under the authority of the Bible. The message of Scripture is the only authority it acknowledges; neither reason nor tradition nor church is accorded any normative position. What it subscribes to exclusively it gives itself to ever so thoroughly. Evangelicals study the Bible over and over, through and through. It is constantly being approached for inspiration as well as for the declaration of truth. They cannot get enough of it; their confidence in the authenticity and power of its message is profound. Typically, they believe it should be interpreted literally, sometimes mostly propositionally, but in other cases more existentially. Even those who interpret it in more dramatic or poetic or historical categories, take it very seriously, indeed as proclaiming an urgent message.

(2) It follows that Evangelicals live with a high degree of certainty. What they know, they know for sure. Arrogance of claim this is not, rather it is confidence in the power of God to transmit His address to people through unimpeachably clear communication. As we will see, some understand the connection in more rational terms and others in more existential terms. But whatever the particular route to knowledge of God may be, the conviction of the reality acknowledged or known is ever so solid and strong. In most cases, openness to consideration of alternative interpretations exists, therefore a willingness to engage in dialogue and explore the truth with others. Nevertheless, EPs "shall not be moved," staking everything on the divine revelation and informed by its message to them.

(3) A high degree of personal intensity prevails among EPs. The Lord's business is indeed serious business. It is made so by God's grace, Christ's saving death, and the desperate condition of sinful humanity. These being matters of the utmost significance, the Christian is rightly a dedicated, devout, disciplined person. One is to be aware of his calling and on the tips of his toes at all times to hear the Lord's voice and respond obediently. The Christian life is a busy existence, one characterized by a sense of the gravity and urgency of the task. Thus, the EP "wears his religion on his sleeve," is ready, even quick, to talk about it, reacts to everything in Christian categories, and forsakes any sense of the light or humorous or casual whenever calling and opportunity coincide. Everything in life is measured by its importance to God's service.

(4) A clear sense of personal identity is a distinguishing badge of EP men and women. They know who they are—Christians, children of the King, followers of Christ, the called and commissioned, forgiven sinners, bearers of the truth, Spirit-led. witnesses. They are not people who "happen to be" such-and-such. Their identity is definitively shaped by direct action of the Lord Himself and their own deliberate response to Him. Before they are fathers or mothers, businessmen or teachers, Republicans or Democrats, they are the Lord's own. This makes for a deep security in their self-understanding and their roles with other people and in the various frames of life. It also makes for clear goals. One knows what he or she is to be doing under all circumstances, or at least how to find out rather handily, through prayer and Bible study.

(5) A strong sense of responsibility to others is equally characteristic of the EP style of living. The EP is not a hermit nor an isolationist nor one who lives for self-gratification. Rather one is put here for a purpose which has to do with other people. This responsibility to others may take any number of forms, including witnessing to a lost person about the condition of his soul, leading the spiritually blind or perverse to see the truth, sharing the contagion of the Holy Spirit's presence, and giving a cup of cold water to a thirsty person in Christ's name. The life of faith is not a commodity to be hoarded but a quality to be shared. The Christian is not called or commissioned in general, but impelled to undertake specific tasks. There are millions of people in need of God—God's truth, God's salvation, God's comfort, God's concern, and much more that He yearns to provide.

Evangelical Protestants, thus, are a people to be taken seriously, just as they themselves take seriously their walk of faith. They are often a noisy, visible people, characteristically a bold, determined, aggressive people. Others in the society may founder on the shoals of an uncertain existence; not they. Others may wander aimlessly; not they. Others may take life in stride, passing from one day to the next; not they. Others may cast about to discover the truth in deep seas which are stingy in disgorging their fruits; not they. EPs are an entrusted, empowered, emboldened, inspirited, commissioned lot who are earnestly setting out to carry on the work of the Lord. There is no better simple example of this than an ordinary conversation with an EP. Up to a certain point, pleasantries and conventions may be exchanged. Everyday matters of business or pleasure may be the subjects under discussion. But after a while, the EP turns the conversation deliberately toward the Master's business. At that point, it is as though a curtain had fallen. Light, humorous tones give way to earnest, urgent ones. The open quest yields to dealing with authoritative questions and answers. The EP is in his element; all the rest is preliminary and tangential to the real purposes of life. Incidentally, this highly intense expression of EP faith is proportionately larger among northerners than among Southerners who wear their certainty somewhat more lightly.

To summarize: Evangelical Protestantism rests on a theology of unmediated encounter. The "flight" of God to the person is "non-stop." He or she lives under the authority of the Bible, with bold certainty, much personal intensity, a clear sense of identity, and a strong sense of responsibility to others. Some will observe that in many ways this description sounds a great deal like classical English Puritanism. But it differs theologically from Puritanism in being more "vertically" than "horizontally" oriented in that it is mostly preoccupied with relation to God rather than concerned with moral and liturgical practice. Yet the tone of the two is basically similar. In both cases attitudes of seriousness, urgency, and dutifulness are representative.

This mild comparison and contrast with Puritanism suggests the mention of two other comparisons, both sharper, within the Protestant family toward the goal of illuminating the evangelical version of Protestantism. Classical Protestantism, of the traditional Lutheran and Calvinist sorts, diverges in acknowledging that forms mediate—the "flight" is "direct" rather than "non-stop"—and in taking a more gradualist, long-range perspective on the accomplishment of God's will in life. This spirit is illustrated by their greater ecumenical sense; they live with the conviction that no group has a corner on truth or responsibility, so all learn and work together, and finally defer to God's accomplishing His own goals even without human responsiveness, if necessary. Liturgical Protestantism, typified by the Episcopal Church (but touching also the Lutheran and even the Methodist traditions) places much stock in the stability of the Church's very existence and therefore somewhat less on individual responsibility and accountability. Because it sees the Christian life as epitomized in corporate worship, making use of the richest and most generative forms it can find in the tradition or can create, it comes down squarely on the side of "direct flights" from heaven to earth. Neither Classical nor Liturgical lives with so much certainty and intensity or so clear a sense of identity and personal responsibility as does Evangelical. Answerability and accountability to God, both prominent attitudes with Puritanism and EP, are recessive in Classical and Liturgical forms of Protestantism. The former two "know more" and effectively bridge the gap between God and people.

General characterizations and comparisons aside, we turn now to four particular versions of Evangelicalism in the American South which express its diversity. They are: (1) truth-oriented EP, rightly called "fundamentalist"; (2) conversion-oriented EP, "evangelistic"; (3) spiritually-oriented EP, "devotional"; (4) service-oriented EP, "ethical." All four have deep roots in southern Christianity, and the first three attract large numbers. It should not be overlooked that a denomination may give evidence of incorporating two or three, or even all four, of these orientations. Likewise an individual may embody two or three. But the fact remains that all four varieties are present in popular southern Protestantism. The common confusion of "fundamentalist," "evangelical," and "evangelistic" makes this point as well as any, while at the same time indicating how often generalizations are made which obscure the fact of diversity.

(1) Truth-oriented EP sees as the essence of Christianity the preaching and practice of the divinely revealed truth of the Bible. It is, accordingly, rationalistic. What is revealed is a series of propositions, laws, and facts which are to be given assent or subscribed to. It follows that EP of this sort wherever found will be "tough." It is not open to dialogue, because it accredits a didactic, not a dialogic, approach to the truth. Its goal then is to build true, pure—"correct"—Christianity and to expose and undermine false teachings and corrupt churches and opinions. Institutional examples of this version are Bob Jones University and its orbit of churches, Tennessee Temple College and its sphere of influence, the Churches of Christ (in their considerable variety), and a number of independent Baptist and sectarian churches.

Truth-oriented EP is rightly referred to as fundamentalist, in that it teaches absolute truth and requires from its members solid subscription to truths as taught. It is given to testing and proving. In other words, standards can be applied, and should be applied, to determine who is faithful to the true teachings. The faithful are identifiable, identified, and accepted. Others are excluded. Churches so inclined are sectarian; they withdraw from falsity wherever it is promulgated. Typically EP groups of this sort are quick to find fault with others and to bond themselves with others only after close and continuing inspection of the others' views. Independency and separatism run strong; cooperation and dialogue are rare.

(2) Conversion-oriented EP interprets the seeking and finding of personal salvation as the essence of Christianity. It gives enormous energies to evangelism, that is, to making individuals aware of their eternally lost condition before God and to acquainting them with the pardon of sins available through accepting Christ as Savior. Their goal is to bring about every individual's new status before God in the experience of conversion. Each person's history is viewed as a telescoping of all history into two eras, a kind of personal B.C. and A.D., before and after the experience of salvation, since one "passes from death unto life" in the event of conversion.

In EP of this type, a tragic separation divides every individual from God. There is no effective relation between them because of the person's sins and sinfulness. But Christ's atoning death, when its benefits are appropriated in faith, reconciles God and the person. This happens through a conscious and deliberate choice-response on the individual's part. From that point forward, the saved person lives with *assurance*. "Assurance" is the key trait of conversion-oriented EP as "tough" is in the case of truth-oriented EP. The converted person knows he or she is saved and is identified to self and others in that way.

The Southern Baptists are conspicuously the best example of this variety. Their animating force is evangelism, the task of saving souls, abroad as well as at home. But a number of sects also practice this approach to Christian responsibility. Revivalism is a commonly used technique for bringing about the desired results; wherever revivals are held, you may be sure that the conversion experience is a high priority. Finally, it should be noted that as we move rightward from truth to conversion—and, later, still further—a lessened sectarian spirit prevails. If conversion-oriented EPs are not ecumenical, they are also not isolationists and may even be quite cooperative, especially with others for whom the conversion of lost people is the heart of the faith.

(3) Spiritually-oriented EP is less sectarian still and can hardly be termed radical. Rather than "tough" or "assured" it is "expressive." Instead of being "hard" (truth) or "pointed" (conversion), its position is "soft." This is devotional religion dwelling on and living by the Lord's intimate and constant presence. For EPs of this sort the distance between God and people is greatly narrowed; at least to those who are attuned and open, the Lord is very near. He fills your heart with sweet peace and joy. He empowers you through prayer to overcome temptation, to live in communion with His Spirit, and to know His guidance through every event and decision of life. The goal of Christianity, accordingly, is to experience Him for the sake of knowing that He and His joy are what life is all about, and so as to share this contagion with others who are missing out on the essence of Christianity and, indeed, the true purpose and meaning of life.

This version of EP shows up in quite a wide variety of Protestant varieties. Old-fashioned southern Methodism represents a mild form of this posture of faith. The mainline Black Protestant churches, Baptist and Methodist principally, deserve classification here. They practice expressive, enthusiastic, joyful, soulful faith. Contrary to much popular opinion they do not stress salvation from guilt, sin, and hell, choosing rather to magnify the accessibility and power of "the Lord's intimate and constant presence." Of a more extremist nature are the charismatic and pentecostal peoples who are found in a number of sects. For them not only is God present and active, he leaps the gap between the natural and supernatural to generate the healing of body or mind or to enable the Spirit-possessed person to "speak in tongues." In all such instances, the supernatural does not penetrate and direct the natural, it overwhelms it and abrogates it.

(4) Service-oriented Evangelical Protestantism is far less widely practiced in the South than the other three varieties but it is just as authentically regional. Christians of this kind operate with the conviction that what God wills is that people should be reconciled to each other and live with dignity in a society of mutual support and concern. In the South historically that has often translated as dedication to the establishment of civil rights for black people, to constructive black-white racial relations, and to the improvement of the lot of the poor and outcast, "red-necks" as well as Negroes.

Their goal is to reconcile all people as God's creation to each other, irrespective of biological, cultural, or economic circumstances. Undertakings of this sort have proven to be particularly unpopular and difficult given the development of southern history, and their practitioners often labelled "radical." There is something right about this characterization of service-oriented EPs. They are a "determined" company of Christians. Typically working quietly and gradualistically, they show set jaws; they embody qualities of patience, resilience, and resourcefulness.

Two dramatic examples of this bear mention, although it should be pointed out that many individuals working "quietly and gradualistically" are dotted all around the southern landscape. In 1942, the Reverend Dr. Clarence Jordan began the Koinonia Farm near Americus, Georgia. He felt a calling to demonstrate that black people and white people could live together in the heartland of the Deep South. The several families who lived under the same roof and tilled the land together even practiced economic communalism. The news that they experienced a great deal of harassment and ostracism over the years (before 1964 especially) surprises no one.

The Reverend Will D. Campbell, Yale-trained Baptist preacher from south Mississippi, looms large as a second example. A true maverick, Campbell has worked tirelessly as an itinerant servant of God for the past quarter-century as he has endeavored to minister to the outcasts and the deprived, such as the poor, black people, red-necks, and convicts—the wretched of the southern earth. For him too what God yearns to see is people realizing their worth, granted basic rights and opportunities, and living harmoniously with human beings from all social classes, races, and points of view.

Recapitulating, we note that four distinct versions of one family of Protestant Christianity exist and are at home in the culture of the American South. (1) Truth-oriented EPs see religion as something you *believe*; its sacrament words are "New Testament Church" and "Word of God." (2) Conversion-oriented EPs see religion as something you *get* and *have*; its distinctive sacrament word is "born again." (3) Spiritually-oriented EPs see religion as something you *be* (are); "the Lord is in my heart," (4) Service-oriented EPs see religion as something you *do*; "love your neighbor." It is important to call attention again to the fact that while these are identifiable and distinctive forms, they are far from being discrete. A denomination or an individual may manifest the characteristics of two or three or even all four of them. Yet, one is likely to be dominant, standing as the animating principle, with the others recessive. It also belongs to the evangelical mentality, especially on the left, to claim and flaunt "distinctives" which set them apart and highlight their purity.

We need to return to a question touched on earlier, namely, whether Evangelical Protestantism so described is a distinctly southern phenomenon or, conversely, whether what is described here is not merely "popular southern Protestantism" without any precise reference to the historic family of Protestantism called Evangelical. I believe the issue is rather easily laid to rest, along these lines. These four regional varieties are all evangelical in the broad sense and properly are classified in that historic and world-wide grouping of Protestant Christians.

Yet there are some pecularities which set off southern forms. One is a contrast of southern EP, especially of its most popular and representative variety, the conversion-oriented, with mainline contemporary Evangelicalism in the North and West of the United States, the kind typified by Fuller Theological Seminary, Wheaton and Calvin Colleges, and Inter-Varsity Christian Fellowship (a nationwide ministry to campuses). Southern EP has a tendency to make its intensity occassional and goal-directed. That is, it modulates the Christian responsibility to a higher key, pushes it up to a higher plane, *on occasion*—on the occasion of an individual's or a congregation's efforts to convert the lost. In other words, it is task-oriented. Otherwise the religious life is lived rather matter-of-factly (a description meant to describe rather than negatively evaluate). By contrast, mainline northern EP, a sort which is a bit "out of place" when seen in the South, makes the religious life a combination of intense, serious, and conscious all the time, or at any rate just below the surface and easily called forward any time. It is a more disciplined and life-comprehending mode of Christian expression. In a peak religious experience, the southern EP becomes busy, vocal, and promotional. The mainline northern variety, instead, gets serious, quiet, intense, humorless, sacrificial, and patient. Perhaps the service-oriented type is the one of the four southern versions with which it shares the most. But the mainline northern variety outstrips the latter in its more explicit vertical awareness, exemplified as a desire to make Christians and to defend the authority of Scripture. In other words mainline northern EP is "tough" and "assured" as well as "determined," but in ways which mark it off from such southern examples as Bob Jones fundamentalism and Southern Baptist revivalism.

Another regional distinctiveness has to do with ethics, specifically the ways in which personal piety is translated into public responsibility. It should be remarked that all four southern varieties are apolitical, which is to be distinguished from being necessarily unpolitical or antipolitical. Even service-oriented EPs express their profound ethical concern in apolitical ways, through personal example, one-to-one ministry, and informal association. Their altruistic behavior is second to none, but it is not accomplished through altering social arrangements or assaulting corporate structures. In the southern manner, it is personal, one-to-one, associative. Where notably political tacks are taken, they occur outside EP, in the southern denominations kin to the northern mainline, Presbyterian, Methodist, Episcopal, and Quaker—and Roman Catholic.

But, reference to southern EP as apolitical in no way implies that it has no concern for or involvement in the public life of society. It does have, in several ways. One is through the support of institutions of higher learning. The record of the southern denominations in founding and maintaining colleges and universities is impressive. They have been at it since antebellum days, and the number of the sponsored institutions is large. Considering the lack of financial resources among most of the southern rank-and-file until quite recently, you have to conclude that their investments in colleges were given high priority. Obviously, one of the major incentives has been to prepare men for the ministry and train the young people in their own communions. But, to the extent that these have been colleges and not indoctrination stations—and that is most of the time, they have taken the risks entailed by free critical inquiry and seen the value of education to the society at large. After making certain allowances in some cases, you can only interpret the establishment of church-related colleges as a foray into the public realm and desire to serve it in ways which transcend church boundaries.

Second, the mounting of numerous crusades against the manufacture, sale, and consumption of alcoholic beverages has been a primary way in which southern piety, characteristically apolitical, has been active in the public realm. From the 1880s forward, the EP churches have displayed a relentless vigor in endeavoring to rid southern society of intoxicating beverages. In beginning to do so, they broke with their earlier customs of enjoying the drinking of spirits (beer and wine to a smaller degree), and with their tradition of minding their own spiritual business, leaving political matters to the political arena. Since then, on this issue especially, they have been up to their barrel rims in politics. In addition to home and church teaching against the use of intoxicating beverages, they have run candidates on anti-booze platforms, developed an extensive local option system, and organized referendums to express their views. Notwithstanding the classification of drinking as a matter of personal rather than social ethics, the activities of the EP denominations in prohibiting or controlling alcohol's place in society have propelled their piety squarely into the middle of social responsibility.

The conduct of the Georgian who recently moved out of the White House looms as a third route from piety to public involvement. Mr. Carter is only the most famous in a long line of southern EPs who have declared their conviction that God was calling them to serve Him through a political vocation. Young people in many of the churches are encouraged to discern whether God wants them to be "good Christians in government." Most often that counsel is intended to mean that clean, honest, sober people who are in position to render Christian influence, and even to use their fame as leverage for winning lost souls to Christ, should work to bring about that opportunity for service. Mr. Carter seems to have moved beyond that interpretation of the good Christian in politics, a fact which qualifies his identification with the ranks of a typical southern EP. For, in addition to being a prayerful, pious, and witness-bearing individual, he believes in a Christian social ethic which translates piety into corporate concerns like justice and human rights and into the transformation of massive social structures. Mr. Carter's posture is indeed atypical among southern EPs. Nevertheless there is a certain instinct deep within southern piety to enter the political sphere, thereby to render service to God. It is not surprising that this instinct is rarely found among truth-oriented EPs who tend to be comprehensively sectarian; it may come as something of a shock that service-oriented EPs often avoid such entanglements. Conversion- and spirituality-EPs are the breeds most likely to enter the public forum.

A fourth, somewhat subtle, example must complete our illustrative list. It has to do with curtailing free inquiry, whether in the public schools or in the colleges. From time to time in more rural or otherwise culturally homogeneous areas, southern EPs with worried and even seared consciences will do battle with the teaching of biological evolution, the critical study of the text of the Holy Bible, use of a modern translation of the Bible, or open examination of an alien social system such as Communism. When this occurs, there is often more astir than mere theological or patriotic orthodoxy. The populace which so protests does so in part because of its intuition, not even formulated, much less pronounced, that challenges to prevailing ideologies threaten to undermine social convention, order, and values. Seeing far beyond their noses into rather sophisticated sociological areas, such Christian leaders struggle to preserve the consensus which they believe has made theirs a wholesome, God-fearing society. In this subtler, more complex way, as well as the three more concrete instances we previously noted, southern EP religion bursts its banks of piety to spill over into the social-political lowlands lying beyond. It is fascinating to note that this is a frequent, and predictable, pattern of behavior among the most sectarian southern EPs, those oriented to the truth.

At some length now we have been observing how Evangelical Protestantism, southern style(s), has transcended its individualism, its strongly vertical orientation, and its yearning for purity, to involve itself in that wider secular order which forms the larger context of living. That it has been doing so for a long time with an admirably rich variety is a point badly in need of making since it has been so often overlooked or not seen. Nevertheless the most frequently offered criticism of southern EP still has much validity: that, failing to see that society (and its culture) is not coterminous with the individuals who comprise it, aborts its ministry by not assuming responsibility for bringing God's will to bear on the corporate structures which made such heavy impact on lives. From the sectarianism of the truth party all the way to the Anabaptist values of many of the service people, southern EP defines its responsibility chiefly as being to individuals. From its own perspectives, it either has no responsibility to society as such or it discharges that responsibility by ministering to individuals. Because of its strength, even predominance, in regional culture a great deal that historically has been assumed to be the task of the Christian Church goes unattended, or is left to the minority who comprise the vigorous sector of the mainline denominations.

A recent piece of research has highlighted this feature of southern EP. Earle, Knudsen, and Shriver, three sociologists of religion, undertook a thorough study of the relation between religion and society in Gastonia, North Carolina. In *Spindles and Spires*, they disclose their findings that two issues dominate and have dominated the community for many decades: race relations and the unionization of labor in the community's many textile mills (and other factories).[2] On the former issue, attitudes are shown to have become rather open, with the churches standing as a mild force in the improvement of black people's lot and relations between the races. With respect to unionization, little has been accomplished and the churches have generally opposed any change in that direction. The difference in the roles of the churches in the two cases is instructive:

> The matter boils down to a greater ease with personal than with structural relations. Blacks are a people, an alienated people, who nevertheless have been acquaintances, even friends, of many of their white neighbors. Whites' awareness of the multiple deprivations suffered by many blacks occasions an uneasy conscience. Moreover, much of the needed amelioration can take place at the personal, substructural

---

[2]John R. Earle, Dean D. Knudsen, and Donald W. Shriver, *Spindles and Spires* (Atlanta: John Knox Press, 1975).

level, through increased concern and kindness. Unions, and the process of unionization, are something else again. Gastonia blacks are people whose deprivations, when perceived as such, are largely economic, it is true. But labor unions build the case for contending with this condition through an unfamiliar rendering of an abstract principle, justice. In a nutshell, the labor movement is institutional, not personal, and, further, bespeaks an invasion from the outside by one sector of the American population whose image is dominantly non-Anglo-Saxon. In the final analysis, ethnicity may be more important in Gastonia than race, if for no other reason than that the ethnics are not "our kind of people." But the more salient explanation here is that highly organized, structural arrangements for implementing ideology are foreign to Gastonian ideology. What *Spindles and Spires* makes clear in a variety of connections is that Gastonians function with a muscular sense of individualism—and by implication with an anemic understanding of corporate or structural arrangements. The authors' data reveal that the church members tend to advocate change, believing that is the church's responsibility, but change is interpreted as the influence of the aggregate of changed individuals, and not in structural terms.[3]

How to bring its message to bear on a society (qua society) for which it has won the right to be responsible is indeed Evangelicalism's chief problem, and blind spot, in the South. But it shows some sensitivity to that need and has found some ways of effectuating that responsibility.

Earlier we looked at some issues which claimed the attention of one conscientious southern pietist with the expectation that doing so would reveal something of "southern soul." Now I propose to continue that same effort by making a "spiritual appeal"—doing a little preaching, colloquially stated. This brief reflection, if it succeeds in addressing the real situation, will highlight regional shortcomings, weaknesses, and blind spots on the one hand, and regional resources and capacities on the other. It is offered as an indirect form of analysis, but additionally as a

---

[3]Review of *Spindles and Spires* by Samuel S. Hill, Jr., *Religious Studies Review* 4:1 (January 1978):17.

challenge to growth in depth by the southern religious community.

A number of points of access, or tender spots, exist among southern Christians. To begin with, they are a deeply religious people, by intention and in sensibility, and have been so at least from the antebellum period. They take a supernaturalistic view of reality and life readily, almost instinctively it would appear. Observers from Frederick Law Olmsted in the 1850s down to Jimmy Carter watchers have been struck by the powerful hold on the people of the region exercised by a Christian metaphysic and notions of the providential ordering of events, but most of all, the conviction that God is very near each person to give and to require. Seeing truth in a Christian framework, almost as a matter of course, it sometimes seems, they are uncommonly open to a consideration of the Christian message. Church attendance, respect for the minister and his office, uncritical subscription to the authority of the Bible, responsiveness to theological language, the promise of heaven and the threat of hell, and moral bans on a number of practices such as drinking and dancing, are still prominent aspects of the behavior of Southerners. Millions of them, including many who are inactive in church as such, resonate to "God-talk." It is often remarked that the American South is the best place in Christendom for doing theology. The people there do know what theological language points to; or at least they know it is serious business and that they had better listen.

Emotional appeals are still effective. A preacher or dedicated lay person can count on being heard and responded to when such urgent matters as the evangelization of the whole world or the relief of human distress resulting from famine or flood are presented. Generosity with donations of money is often amazing. It is true that some brow-beating or exploitation can be perpetrated on a people who are responsive at their best but gullible at their worst. More often than not, however, those who appeal and those who heed are discerning and have integrity. To a remarkable degree, the southern religious community, especially EPism, is willing to part with its money—often not especially plentiful—in the name of a good cause. As impressive as any detail in this picture is the number of men so disposed. Religion is not a feminine business in the American South. A huge number of men take active parts in church life and give their money generously. Stereotypically speaking, however, it is not amiss to characterize religion of this sort as "feminine" in that it is soft, responsive, charitable, and generous.

The warm humanity of much southern religion is inevitably tied to the general experience of the people of the region. As is well known, the history of the South has been different from that of the rest of the nation. Its people have come face to face with poverty, defeat, and low esteem in the eyes of others as no other Americans have. But such trying circumstances has been accompanied by and helped produce many positive qualities. Anguish over low economic, educational, and cultural achievements have been coordinated with a strong sense of rootedness, healthy family relationships, and a high degree of sociability. These and other painfully or joyfully real encounters with life have contributed to Southerners' "doing a lot of living." No doubt, their embracing of religious perspectives which magnify guilt, hope, fellowship, joy, simplicity, reverence, confidence, and expressiveness are rooted in the folk character of a society drawn together and to each other by a great many destructive forces. It is also true that a great many of these forces have been largely of their own making. That is to say, southern religion has had to come to terms with the seamy side of life because so much of southern living has been seamy. After all is said and done, the racial situation of the South has dominated its life from 1790 until recently. It is apparent that there is little good which can be said about "white over black," that is, the record of the superior group in its dealings with and provisions for their black fellow Southerners. A large part of southern whites' "doing a lot of living" is bound up with the co-existence of black and white people on conditions set by the white society, first slavery, then segregation, but always the kind of deep alienation which results from one group regarding another as "those other people." Among the ruling whites it would be natural for guilt and moral anguish to prevail and produce the need for forgiveness. For their part blacks have turned to Christianity (since 1800, rarely before that) saliently as a source of hope, comfort, sustenance, and assurance, and, more often than whites knew, as incentive for change. The main point here is that in quite divergent ways, white and black Southerners have needed religion badly and have turnd to it for answers. In both instances the Lord had to be very near, whether as judge and redeemer or as consolation and mainstay. People from outside the region are amazed at the innocence and profoundity of Southerners' experience of the Lord; a glance at their history provides more than a little illustration.

This is a spotty, dark, ugly record of a situation wherein cruelty and even extermination have been practiced. The damage done to Afro-

Americans—and to themselves—by "white over black" policies and underlying attitudes is incalculable. It was only worsened by a long desperate search to justify slavery and segregation on Christian terms: (a) God willed that the Africans be brought here so that they could be Christianized; (b) the Bible speaks approvingly of slavery; (c) slavery is a necessary evil; (d) slaveholders must practice Christian ethics in dealing with their human property; (e) some are meant to belong to a class of hewers-of-wood and drawers-of-water; (f) the Christians' responsibility is to save the souls of black folk, not to liberate them, body and soul. A harsh story and dark record indeed, and religion is an inextricable part of it.

Yet, as a number of blacks and whites alike believe, even so horrible an arrangement as "white over black" can issue in some constructive good. One dramatic illustration of this which says a great deal about life in the South dates from a strike on a state university campus by black cafeteria workers in 1969. They were protesting a wage structure which fell below the standards of the state of which this university was an agency, a "revolting development" to be sure. Tensions were great. The threat of violence was enough to require the presence of national guardsmen on the campus. But severe activities were averted, in part through an old friendship between some black people and some white people in a neighboring county. It happened this way.

A thoughtful member of the university staff (a white woman), having initiated dialogue with leaders of the striking black workers, discovered that one of them had grown up in a sharecropper's family on the farm of a (white) man who had become a prominent politician in the state. A phone call to him elicited a recollection of this black woman from her childhood days and that she and her family were "mighty fine folks." One thing led to another—it helped that this state leader was a relative of the governor—as the striving factions were brought together. The settlement of the strike and the expanded protection of workers' rights which came about in fairly short order were accomplished with the aid of this turn of events. It has long been a fact that black and white people have known each other in the South, have shared many experiences, and quite often have been friends. That is one of the South's most basic resources for good.

Vincent Harding, a major southern black spokesman, has offered a penetrating analysis of the "uses of the Afro-American past" which

Southerners are in the best position to exploit among all Americans.[4] After noting that insensitivity to the oppressed, the wretched of the earth, is a national blind spot, he moves constructively to look at the black experience in America—which is one major portion of the total American experience. It possesses the power to equip America with eyes to see reality. He hopes that that sight will produce action, toward liberty, justice, and opportunity for all. The kinds of sensitivity displayed by Harding have often been generated by the history of southern society and by the kind of moral and religious piety which abound in so many southern breasts. Cause and cure, problem and solution, sinners and redeemers, the ugly and the beautiful—such antinomies are fundamental to the southern soul. Each side must be seen, and the dialectical relation between them, if the shape of popular southern piety is to be understood. Fortunately, there are tender spots, points of access, resources, and capacities constituent of the southern experience.

A final stratagem I choose to employ under the rubric of spiritual appeal is a brief apologetic program. Apologetics is an old science in Christianity, the presentation of a reasoned case in its behalf as a recommendation of it. As before, the purpose in this is two-fold: to call forth a response from the church in the South; and to provide an indirect description of popular piety in the region. Concerning the latter, I hope to indicate some strengths of character which Christianity possesses (in my interpretation) which are not standard components of the southern representation of it (to say the least, in some instances).

Christianity is not exhausted by grasping any one or two of its layers or ways of construing its meaning. It is a many-splendored thing, a comprehensive depiction of reality; accordingly it has to do with outer history and inner history, body and spirit, the past and the present, and a great many other complementarities. It follows that Christianity should prize search, quest, movement, dialectic, paradox, mystery, irony, and humor, as well as certainty and boldness of conviction and earnestness of spirit. The Christian faith is a force with direct implications for both the public and private spheres of life, for objective and subjective dimensions of experience, for both the corporate and individual arenas. Therefore, it deserves to be accorded critical distance as well as related to with

    [4]Vincent Harding, "Uses of the Afro-American Past" in *The Religious Situation,* 1969, ed. Donald R. Cutler (Boston: Beacon Press, 1969), pp. 829-40.

intimacy. Christians therefore do well to work and pray, to study and feel, to speak of our faith and my faith, to see God's hand in secular affairs as well as through spiritual institution, to view religion as subtle and indirect as well as personal and existential.

Speaking personally, I find several criteria acutely valid for discriminating judgment and effective apologetics. (1) Is love embodied and promoted by your particular belief and practice, "love" understood in its Christian meaning as "creative good will"? (2) Does your understanding of Christian meaning get you all the places you should go? That is, does it begin to do justice to the richness of Christian claims and their complex relation to the complexity of human life? (3) How does your view stand up in the light of public scrutiny? Is it as penetrating and authentic when assessed in the light of historically accredited validations of meaning (according to Christianity) as your private judgments or "leadings of the heart" suggest that it is? (4) Does your view address the great facts of life boldly, directly, adequately, centrally, such profound issues as death, evil, ambiguity, and complexity? (5) Does it generate a wide enough range of responses to correspond to the wideness of Christianity's scope? I refer to: joy, celebration, incentive, direction, humility, openness, challenge, comfort, affirmation, disturbance, guilt, forgiveness, and all the rest that make up the drama of life? Do you dance as a consequence of your faith? Does it also entail serious reflection? Does it even go beyond them to impel dutiful responsibility?

This brief excursus into apologetics may manage transparency to what I intend: (a) to show piety in as deep a form as this person can presently grasp; (b) to call southern Christians to be even more pious than they are through seeing that the faith is even grander than they affirm it to be.

In my first serious analysis of the popular religion of the South, written nearly fifteen years ago, I spoke of it as one footnote in the massive history of Christianity.[5] Quantitatively, that may still be a valid observation. But to describe it so is to diminish at least its colorfulness and potential. It is distinctive, it is a partialized embodiment of the Christian tradition (aren't they all?), and it is not a form of the faith likely to be attractive and effective to a culturally diverse civilization over a long

---

[5]Samuel S. Hill, Jr., *Southern Churches in Crisis* (New York: Holt, Rinehart and Winston, 1966), p. 211.

period of time. Yet it packs a great deal of authenticity and wields enormous influence. For reasons like these the shape and shapes of popular southern piety deserve a fairer analysis and better hearing than they have usually enjoyed. This essay and its companion pieces are offered in the hope of accomplishing those objectives.